GRAHAM

crackers

Fuzzy Memories,

Silly Bits, and Outright Lies

By Monty Python's
Graham Chapman

Compiled by Jim Yoakum

CAREER
PRESS

Copyright © 1997 by Jim Yoakum

GRAHAM CRACKERS
ISBN 1-56414-334-1 $14.99
Cover design by Tom Phon
Typesetting by Eileen Munson
Printed in the U.S.A. by Book-mart Press

To order this title by mail, please include price as noted above, $2.50 handling per order, and $1.50 for each book ordered. Send to: Career Press, Inc., 3 Tice Road, P.O. Box 687, Franklin Lakes, NJ 07417.

Or call toll-free 1-800-CAREER-1 (in NJ and Canada: 201-848-0310) to order using VISA or MasterCard, or for further information on books from Career Press.

Library of Congress Cataloging-in-Publication Data

Chapman, Graham, 1941?-1989
    Graham crackers : fuzzy memories, silly bits, and outright lies /
by Graham Chapman ; compiled by Jim Yoakum.
        p.   cm.
    ISBN: 1-56414-334-1
    1. Chapman, Graham, 1941?-1989 --Miscellanea.   I. Yoakum, Jim.
II. Title.
PN2598.C27A3   1997
828' .91407--dc21   97-31555
                                                                        CIP

Contents

Part Two: Silly Bits

Part Three: Outright Lies

By John Cleese

Graham: A dear friend, a lazy bastard

Graham was a dear friend of us all, despite the fact that he was a lazy, freeloading bastard with only the most tenuous grasp of reality. In fact, in his twilight years he lost interest in the real world completely. If you don't believe me, ask his accountants. Consequently, making up lies came very easily, and indeed unintentionally, to him.

Actually, *I* had the brilliant idea of writing an utterly mendacious biography several years before Graham stole it from me. Never mind, he did after all need the money.

Now this book appears to be an attempt to extract further revenues from *my* idea. However, as some of the royalties will go to David Sherlock, who put up with Graham for many years and richly deserves a bit of compensation, I could not, therefore, recommend this book more strongly.

—John Cleese, August 1997

By Eric Idle

Graham Chapman: The youngest Python

Graham Chapman was a very doctory type of person. Lest that should inspire confidence in the unwary, never forget his caveat: "Doctors are only ex-medical students." You have been warned.

Graham has quite cleverly now become the youngest Python.

As the rest of us soldier on into late middle age, the late Graham Chapman—he was famous for being late—is, alas, still dead. But not forgotten. At the last Python meeting, we even gave him a vote. "All right, Graham," we said, "One knock for yes, two for no." He abstained. Which was fine. Since he never really abstained very much in his life.

The sadness of his early demise is still with us. The malady lingers on. At the 25th Anniversary of Python in Los Angeles, I was with David Sherlock and said how much I missed Graham. "I wish he were here now," I said. "Oh, but he *is*," said David.

"He's in my pocket!" And he produced his ashes! Next night, he sprinkled them over the front row of the audience.

Very Graham. He hated sentimentality. But not sentiment. So perhaps this is okay. He always looked on the Bright Side. He is still available on video, he has a new book out, a new CD, and I believe David still has some ashes left.

—Eric Idle, August 1997

By Terry Jones

Graham, Lemon Curry, and all that

A few words about Graham. Okay, the great thing about Lemon Curry (I'm sorry, *Graham*) was his (*with a melon?*) unpredictability. He would sit there through a Python group "writing" session picking the odd spot on his shoulder (that was when he was going through his semi-nude stage), puffing on his pipe and even—in the bad old days—sipping from a large glass of water which he always kept to hand. We all thought it was part of his obsession with keeping fit, until we discovered it wasn't water.

Lemon Curry. You see! That's exactly what would happen! Just when you weren't expecting it, out would come the *nonsequitur*, which, of course, shouldn't have been there at all (*being a nonsequitur*) but which somehow summed up the whole moment.

Graham's writing, at its best, was like that—it had that enviable quality of giving no evidence of where it came from. *He* was like that, too, except that we all *knew* he came from Leicester, though Graham showed not the slightest sign of having *come* from Leicester. As far as I was concerned, he had come from the moon—an amiable Looney with the gift of conveying enormous reassurance. You always felt it would be all right while Graham was around—whatever "it" was. And then he would be off 'round the bar of the King's House Hotel, Glencoe, determined to kiss everyone in the bar. Which he did. And got into a fight. And got banned from the bar.

I only saw one of Graham's lectures, in New York. I went along wondering what on earth to expect. And, once again, Graham surprised me, this time with the warmth of his humour. It was a mellow Graham looking back happily with an audience of friends—well, they were all friends by the end of the evening.

—Terry Jones, August 1997

"It's"... what, exactly?

Congratulations. By choosing this book you have indeed shown your discerning taste and have made a wise purchase decision.

(Er, you did buy his book, didn't you? I mean, you didn't steal it, or—worse—you're not just loitering around the book store "browsing," are you? Go on, march up to the counter and lay down your hard-earned cash. You won't regret it, I promise you. Go on, I'll wait...dum-de-dum... What? Bought it? Great!)

Anyway, as I was saying, you have made a wise purchase (*all of your friends are going to be terribly jealous*), showing intelligence and savvy far beyond the average book patron. Nevertheless, I am sure that you are asking yourself, "Okay, just what the hell have I paid for here? A book by Graham Chapman? Isn't he *dead*? Or, wait, is this—can it be—perhaps...the long-awaited sequel to Graham's cult classic, A *Liar's Autobiography*?!"

A very wise and sensible question, but the answer is, alas, no.

So what the hell *is* "It," already?

This is a book of bits and bobs. A scrap book. A "last will and testicle," if you will.

It's Graham speaking about his days up to, during, and after Monty Python.

It's Graham on his days pre- and post-A *Liar's Autobiography,* some mere months before his untimely death.

It's unreleased comedy sketches, bits of never-before-seen-but-infamous TV scripts ("Our Show for Ringo Starr," co-written with Douglas Adams).

It's Graham spinning (mostly-true) tales about himself and his friends and their many mad adventures.

It's Keith Moon balanced on a hotel ledge, it's Graham whizzing down a mountain in a gondola-on-skis accompanied by a loony named Zan Fitz-Allen Herbert and a wooden dummy with a rather animated erection.

It's Graham in a carrot suit, it's Graham in the raw, it's Graham up-close, outspoken, and outrageous.

It's intercourse Italian-style!

It's David Hemmings as a hippy Gestapo officer!

It's "*It's.*" It's the Spanish Inquisition. And it's something completely different.

Call it what you will, but it's all of these things.

And if it's not a sequel by intent, I guess it's a sequel by default, and that means it's okay by me.

And why am I writing this tedious introduction about *It?*

Where do I fit into all this nonsense?

My relationship with the late Graham Chapman, the late John Tomiczek,[1] and the-very-much-still-alive David Sherlock began in the worst possible way, with me as a journalist asking them all sorts of nosy questions for a book I was writing about the "Monty Python" television series. Luckily, Graham and family were wise and kind, and they somehow managed to overlook my misguided career path and not only took me into their home, but also into their hearts, their confidences and, eventually, into their lives. I was one of the lucky few who was able to make the insurmountable leap from nosy journalist to family friend. A position I still value today with David.

Following the path of least resistance and the willingness to try something new—sometimes for the sheer unadulterated hell of it—were pretty much the mottoes that guided Graham's life. He once told me that, as a child, he put a chair in the kitchen sink and sat in it for most of a day...just to get a different perspective.

---

1 John was a runaway teenager from Liverpool who had met Graham and gotten an autograph outside a restaurant in London. One night (mid-1970s) Graham had John (who had a bad fever) brought to his home where he treated him (Graham was a doctor). He stayed for several weeks. After John ran away from home several more times, John's father awarded Graham and David custody of John. Graham later adopted John as his ward, and John grew up to become Graham's semi-personal manager. In the early 1990s, John married an American girl but, sadly, died shortly thereafter of heart trouble.

That's probably how he viewed our working relationship, as inconsequential as a chair in the kitchen sink, but I treasure it all the same. And while our professional relationship was relatively short-lived (in the end just a handful of sketches, some script concepts, and a few other things), it was still an intense, invigorating and immensely educational period for me. I feel extremely privileged to ever have known him, and he is one person I know I shall never forget—nor ever, really, quite understand.

But then, *I* never put a chair in the kitchen sink.

—Jim Yoakum, August 1997

Part One

Fuzzy Memories

CHAPTER 1

In the beginning was the word... and the word was "silly"

I first met John Marwood Cleese, probably the funniest man I've ever had the pleasure to know, when I arrived at Cambridge University. At the time, I was trying to join a review society called the Footlights. I suspect Footlights was the real reason I went to Cambridge in the first place, although I told everyone else (including myself) that I'd gone there to study medicine.

Well, John and I joined the Footlights together, and Eric Idle joined about a year after that, so the three of us first knew each other from Cambridge. We three then met Michael Palin and Terry Jones while we were all performing at the Fringe of the Edinburgh Festival one year. As fate would have it, we all ended up writing scripts for a television satire program called "The Frost Report," which was hosted by a gentleman called David Frost.

"The Frost Report" was a live program, which, because it *was* live, had the ability to be topical. Not that it always *was*, but it certainly had that ability. It was, in essence, a disguised sketch show. David would deliver what was referred to as the "CDM" ("Continuous Developing Monologue," though we called it "Cadbury's Dairy Milk") and then would act as *compere*, linking sketches together using awful set-up lines like "Have you ever wondered what it would be like if...?" or "Don't you hate it when...?" The sketches were supposed to be based on a common theme each week, such as "The Frost Report on Crime," "On Banking" or "The Arts." But those were only used as loose definitions, as the sketches could be twisted to suit any subject, really.

On balance, John and I had to write two sketches a week for "The Frost Report," an experience which I quite enjoyed, and I think John did, too, because writing like this made us have to think about different areas and different topics. Although certain themes began to repeat quite a lot. Such as mothers. The appalling Mrs. Cleese/Mrs. Chapman appeared regularly, though I don't think our mothers ever recognized themselves!

"Just a routine inquiry, sir"

Before we "officially" wrote for "The Frost Report," John and I did write a quickie for another David Frost-hosted program called "That Was the Week That Was."[1] It was a 30-second, vaguely anti-police item (drawn partly from my experience with my father, a policeman) based upon their irritating habit of uttering the phrase, "Just a routine inquiry, sir." In the sketch, we had a policeman knock on someone's door and then ask the gentleman who answers it, "Are you Mark James?" The man says, "No," at which point the policeman proceeds to kick the shit out of the man. After he's finished, the policeman salutes him and says, "Just a routine inquiry, sir."

The Renaissansical Mr. Frost

A very modest gentleman, David Frost.[2] His program, if you noticed, was called "The Frost Report," and the credits at the end of the program went: STARRING DAVID FROST in big, huge letters and WRITTEN BY DAVID FROST in even bigger letters. And then the names of about 30 other writers just went whizzing past...

Brooooooouuuummmmppphhhh!!!

...and John, Michael, Terry, Eric and I were amongst those 30 names.

[1] A topical satire program that starred David Frost, William ("The Bed-Sitting Room") Rushton and Roy ("Help!, How I Won The War") Kinnear, among others.
[2] He says, placing tongue firmly in cheek.

Writing, writing, everywhere

The next real writing job I had was on a situation comedy called "No That's Me Over Here," directed by Marty Feldman and starring Ronnie Corbett, who had been one of the principle cast of "The Frost Report." I wrote with Barry Cryer, who had also been on the writing staff of "The Frost Report," although the first series of seven programs we also wrote with Eric Idle.

We quickly discovered that writing as a trio was rather unworkable, particularly as Eric only ever writes on his own. The notion that Barry and I would write two-thirds of it together with Eric writing the other one-third simply never panned out very neatly. But, regardless of any difficulties, the series was quite successful on the independent network, and I believe that Barry and I eventually wrote about 50 of the episodes and enjoyed ourselves immensely.

At the same time as I was writing the first year (13 episodes) of "No That's Me Over Here," John Cleese and I began work on another series called "Doctor in the House," which was based on a successful book by Richard Gordon. The first episode of the series was taken partly from that book and embellished by my experiences from my first days at medical school. That series, too, was a joy to write, mainly because the producer had gathered around him a team of wonderful writers, including John and myself, and whenever we were really short of money we would say, "Let's write another show, shall we!"[3]

---

3 Other writers included Bill Oddie and Graeme Garden, later two-thirds of the surreal comedy troupe/TV program, "The Goodies." Later writers included Graham's long-time companion, David Sherlock.

John Cleese, Terry Jones, Eric Idle, Michael Palin, and myself really got to know each other during that period.[4] We also shared the frustration of taking scripts along to script meetings where they'd be read out by the cast who would laugh quite a lot and then say, "Oh, we can't do that! It's too silly." Or "too filthy." Or "too strange." It seems that they were worried about their "image."

Well, *we* weren't bothered at all about *our* image, mainly because we *hadn't* any image at the time, so we subsequently used quite a bit of this material in the first season of "Monty Python" television shows. And we discovered that all those people had indeed been right. The material *was* "silly" and "filthy" and "strange." Consequentially, it was a hit, and we went over like a charm.

Later, when Terry Gilliam decided that he ought to avoid that rather nasty bit of business in the "Vietnamish" area of the world (very sensible, our Terry), he came over to England where John put him in touch with Michael Palin, Terry Jones, and Eric Idle, who were then working on a children's television program called "Do Not Adjust Your Set."[5] Subsequently all four of them joined John and myself when we were considering doing a new television program which turned out to be "Monty Python's Flying Circus."

---

[4] American animator Terry Gilliam, the soon-to-be sixth Python, was then busy working as a sketch artist for a program called "We Have Ways of Making You Laugh." This series, which starred Frank ("My Word!") Muir, has never been seen. Literally. Due to a labor dispute at the time, the only episode of the show was blacked out as it was transmitted. And it was never videotaped.

[5] An outrageous comedy show that also featured the fabulous Bonzo Dog Doo-Dah Band, one of whose members, Neil Innes, reached a certain level of fame (infamy?) as a member of Eric Idle's band, the Rutles.

CHAPTER 2

A horse, a bucket, and a spoon

The name, "Monty Python's Flying Circus" was, to be honest, sort of foisted upon us by the BBC (British Broadcasting Corp.). We were all busy trying to write the first 13 episodes of the series and weren't desperately keen to stop and worry about what to call the bloody thing. I mean, we were panicking just to get everything done before we went into the studio, so we weren't about to spend a lot of time arguing about titles.

There'd already been suggestions, things like "Owl Stretching Time," "The Toad Elevating Moment," and "Sex and Violence." Terry Jones came up with a nice one—"A Horse, a Bucket, and a Spoon." I must say, I rather liked that one. I never *understood* it, but I liked it. We never agreed on any of these titles because, obviously, they were the ideas of individual members of the group and, being human beings, no one else liked them.

We bow to the bureaucrats

But then the BBC's Head of Comedy, Michael Mills, came into our shed and told us that he wouldn't leave until we had given him a title, and that it had to include the word "circus." He desperately wanted a title as he had to have something to put in the TV magazine, and he said we had to use the word "circus" because the BBC had loosely referred to the six of us wandering around the building as "a circus"[1] and that this word "circus" had appeared on contracts and inter-departmental memos and so on, and in a bureaucracy like that it would have a very expensive process to change all of that paperwork![2] So we thought, "All right, we'll swallow that, we'll use the word 'circus.'"

We added "flying" to it to make it sound less like a real circus and more like something to do with the First World War, and then added "Monty Python" because he sounded like a really bad theatrical agent. Just the sort of guy that might have gotten us together. So that was it. None of us liked it, but none of us hated it. Typical committee decision.

---

[1] Kind of a BBC joke, tee-hee-hee.
[2] It probably would have detracted from the budget of the next show. Kind of a Python joke, tee-hee-hee.

I know, let's write a TV show and get rich!

On balance, we had only about five weeks filming for each series of 13 episodes, usually broken up into one two-week session followed by a three-week session. That meant that we had to write all of the sections that needed to be filmed well in advance, and as we started filming some two months before the studio dates, the majority of the shows had to all be pretty much final scripts. Despite the appearance, or the impression some of our fans might have, this left little time for ad-libbing and gave us no chance whatsoever to be topical.

With "Python," one of our biggest problems was also one of our greatest pluses, one that worked for us in a rather odd way. You see, the BBC didn't pay us very much money at all. And there were *six* of us that had to divide that rather meager amount. As a result, the word "repeat" was especially gratifying. It meant one less sketch we had to actually write and act in. If a sketch could be repeated in a year's time, or maybe two, then that would make our paltry fees at least almost reasonable. Therefore we tended *not* to make things topical, as that would simply date the material and make it *less easy to repeat*. (Are you getting the deep, creative reasoning here?)

Also, on the whole, we didn't emphasize impersonation of political characters of our time. Instead of us picking on, say, a particular politician, we usually picked on politicians in general, for a silly, pompous politician is timeless.

I think that's why "Python" shows are just as effective and funny as when we wrote them. Dead parrots and silly walks *are* timeless, aren't they?

The down-side of all this was that the first season of "Python" was very sketch-oriented, as opposed to what it would later develop into, what with its interweaving of characters and situations. I think that we were too insecure during the first season of "Python" to immediately break away from the confines of the sketch show format. We didn't have the guts to make the bold move right away. Plus it was just quite hard to actually do all that "linking" and we didn't much enjoy it so we just didn't do it.

By the second set of 13 episodes, we *did* manage to get further away from the sketch comedy confines, and we were able to go out on a limb and do some ridiculous piece of nonsense which linked two sketches together. We gradually began to enjoy the process of linking, which lead to the development of shows that were more intricate and bold, more "filmatic" than "televisionatic," as it were.

Travel to glamorous climes and stare at bare bosoms!

We attempted to travel to locations which suited the material that had been created, and would give it as much production value as we could get out of the situation. We eventually got as "exotic" as traveling to Jersey, one of the Channel Isles, which is where the whole of "The Cycling Tour" episode was shot (although it had been written with a nicer location in mind!). All of this effort was designed to help get us away from

Bradford, which was where we began location shooting during the first season. Not that there's anything *wrong* with Bradford, aside from the fact that it's in the north of England and is rather cold and wet.

I think that the main reason we went to Bradford in the first place was that Ian MacNaughton, our director, had a girlfriend there. She (or at least *a* girlfriend of his) even appeared in a couple of "Python" episodes, as the lady standing behind the news agent's counter baring her bosoms. She also did an inextricable strip in another episode. That's because I think part of Ian's "arrangement" with this girlfriend was that she would be filmed doing her "act," and that this would somehow get into the program. Of course, this lady's act wasn't written into the program at all! But he somehow *did* manage to slip in a small portion of her act in an episode.

Not a lot of credit for the success of the "Monty Python" series has been given to Ian, which is a shame, really, as he was a jolly fellow to work with. He had previously worked with Spike Milligan on his television series, which was probably why the BBC thought that Ian would be an appropriate director for us.[3] Unfortunately, due to previous commitments on his part, Ian did not actually direct the first four episodes of "Monty Python" (although he did direct the filmed portions). The

---

[3] That would be in the groundbreaking British television series called "Q." According to Terry Jones, the "Q" series was a definite precursor to "Monty Python." Spike Milligan was also a member (along with Peter Sellers) of the landmark BBC-Radio series, "The Goon Show," back in the 1940s. "The Goon Show" has been cited as being a great influence by most of the Pythons (Eric Idle says that he was less influenced by the Goons). Spike also had a brief cameo in *Monty Python's Life of Brian.*

directing duties for the studio portions of these four episodes fell, instead, to a director named John Howard Davies.

The two were very different in style. John was more clinical and formal and very efficient, while Ian thrived in a more chaotic atmosphere. But he was efficient as well. Ian had a spark of craziness about himself, which we appreciated, and which made him appreciate the bits of idiocy that even some of *us* thought were too idiotic to do! So that was quite good. But his "matey" countenance didn't jibe well with everyone—I think John was especially put off by Ian's tendency to be overtly friendly.

As location filming was usually a matter of long stretches of complete boredom occasionally broken up by short periods of intense activity, Ian and I could often be found spending many pleasant hours in some local hotel bar marinating our brain cells. He and I shared a great love affair with ethanol. Usually all it took was him saying, "Hey, hen, how about a drink?" And soon one drink would lead to the inevitable tray.

CHAPTER 3

Graham pulls it off

or why we didn't get

invited to a lot of

parties

David Sherlock, who contributed this chapter, first met Graham on Ibiza in 1966. They were together until Graham's death in 1989. David was a frequent writing partner of Graham's on two TV series—"Doctor in the House" and "Jake's Journey"—and co-authored A Liar's Autobiography. He also contributed to some "Python" sketches ("Death of Mary, Queen of Scots" and "The Oscar Wilde Sketch") and was the inspiration behind the "Python" character Anne Elk, who had a very interesting theory on the brontosaurus. David and Jim Yoakum collaborated on the screenplay of A Liar's Autobiography and have been working on A Liar's Appendix for many years.

When "Python" was at the height of its popularity, all of England's university towns and cities that had accessible public televisions—in pubs, bars, and hotel lounges—would be besieged by student fans. The crowding in some bars was so bad that, for everyone to see what was happening, they would have to climb onto tables and seats, or even onto someone's shoulders, just so they didn't miss a word.

Even the famously wealthy were reputed to return home every Thursday from wherever they happened to be in the world just to be in front of a TV set. It was rumored that George Harrison, for one, never missed a single show.

During this same time, there were many people who loved to say, "Monty Python? I just don't see what's funny. No, I never watch them." This sometimes extended to the old-school British comedians who considered the Pythons to be upstarts from the universities who had never served a "proper apprenticeship" by "treading the boards," as they called it.

Graham Chapman was one of these reviled writer/performers from Cambridge University. By the time "Python" started, he (and all the others) was well-known as a writer of TV and radio shows. At the start of his career, both he and John Cleese wrote for a BBC radio show called "I'm Sorry, I'll Read That Again." John was also performing in the show and was fast becoming the star.

The BBC was quite insistent that "Python" was to be recorded live. The "boys" were equally insistent it wouldn't be.

It was.

Quite a few of the anti-Python brigade used to enjoy saying, "Of course, what I hate about it is the canned laughter during the show." The "canned laughter" they heard was actually a group of near-hysterical teenage fans of Cleese who were always present at recordings of "I'm Sorry, I'll Read That Again" and who simply followed him (as fans do) to the "Python" studio.

By the second year of "Python," Graham found himself working mainly for television. At one time, he was working on two other major TV shows—"Doctor in the House" and "No That's Me Over Here," which was directed by Marty Feldman and starred a well-known and very talented comedian named Ronnie Corbett.

Ronnie and his wife were both well-known in showbiz (still are) and often gave lavish and well-attended parties for all sorts of lavish and exotic showbiz personalities.

We were all invited to one of these parties one Sunday night. The large Tudorbethan house, with views over a beautiful golf course, was full of the famous and the funny. Graham arrived with myself, his young ward, John Tomiczek, and our tall, dark, and handsome chauffeur, Andrew. Heads turned, but then heads usually turned when Graham went to parties.

We were made very welcome by our hosts and, some gin-and-tonics later, we went to join the happy throng who were assembled in a "baronial" living room which, I believe, had a minstrel's gallery. (Yes, it was *that* sort of a place...) At the grand piano, a lady finished warbling a song from the current revival of "Showboat" (most of the cast were in the audience), and the assembled applauded politely. Then, suddenly, a well-known

New York choreographer, who shall remain nameless, appeared. He grinned and began an agonizingly bad striptease, revealing a string tank-top, complete with paunch. People were muttering and examining their shoes. The guy realized his mistake and just as suddenly motioned for the pianist to finish.

As he did so, there was an audible gasp. The assembled were staring aghast at Graham, seated in his chair (on the arm of which I was balanced), where he had proceeded to quietly drop his trousers and underwear down to his ankles and sat serenely smoking his pipe as though nothing were wrong!

It seemed like forever (although the silence must have lasted for only a few seconds) until, from behind us, appeared Danny La Rue, the famous female impersonator (and partner of Ronnie Corbett). With a flourish, he quickly withdrew a handkerchief from his top pocket and carefully placed it over Graham's naughty bits. "Now you see it," he proclaimed, with all the aplomb of a stage magician. "Now you don't!"

Taking his cue, Graham pulled up his trousers and promptly declared that it was "time for another drink." He'd made his point. The spell was broken, and hysterically relieved party noises once again filled the room.

After a "decent" interval, we left for home. But we were never invited back. I fear that much as Ronnie was fond of Graham, he feared what Graham might try as an encore.

Sometime later, we heard that as the guests were discussing the incident, the wife of a great friend was heard to remark: "Well, I thought it was *very* well-formed..."

Graham in mid-1960s, London.

Graham as a child, early 1940s.

Graham with David Sherlock (1968?), at a party in Belsize Park, London.
Just hours before the infamous "severance of a peony" (see chapter 12).

Still from *Monty Python's The Meaning of Life*. Graham Chapman (left), Eric Idle.

Still from *Monty Python's The Meaning of Life*. Standing left to right: Idle, Cleese, Chapman. Sitting left to right: Palin, Jones.

Still from *Monty Python's The Meaning of Life*. Terry Jones (left), Graham (center).

John Cleese and Michael Palin in "The Fish-Slapping Dance Sketch" (one of Graham's favorites).

Cleese will forever be remembered (much to his chagrin) as the silly-walker in the "Ministry of Silly Walks Sketch" (conceived by Chapman/Cleese, but written by Palin/Jones).

The Pepperpots in action! A recreation of the "Hell's Grannies Sketch" for the film *Monty Python's And Now for Something Completely Different* (Jones and Palin in drag, in foreground).

Terry Jones keeps John Cleese from slicing off a piece of Graham Chapman for complaining about dirty utensils in "The Dirty Fork Sketch," for the film *Monty Python's And Now for Something Completely Different.*

Graham and David Sherlock's adopted son, John Tomiczek, mid-1980s, at the Cannes Film Festival, where *Yellowbeard* was an entry.

Graham at their home in Highgate, London, late 1970s.

Graham and longtime companion and frequent writing partner, David Sherlock, on the set of *Monty Python's Life of Brian* (Tunisia, 1979).

Group shot for *Monty Python's The Meaning of Life*. Standing left to right: Jones, Cleese, Gilliam, Chapman, Idle, Palin.

A horse on skis—Dangerous Sports Club, St. Moritz, early 1980s.

Cleese as Blind Pew in *Yellowbeard*.   Graham as Yellowbeard.

Graham with film producer De Haven and film director Damski aboard the good ship Lady Edith (named after his mother) in a candid shot from *Yellowbeard*.

Graham, signing copies of his cult classic, *A Liar's Autobiography*, Highgate, London, early 1980s.

Graham on stage, Georgia Tech, 1988.

Graham and Jim Yoakum, late 1980s.

CHAPTER 4

Writing for Python: A bit like being at school

The six of us formed four distinct creative groups: I used to write mostly with John Cleese; Michael Palin and Terry Jones wrote together—although they did it quite often in different houses, I can't really fathom how they managed that; Eric Idle wrote on his own; and Terry Gilliam, of course, was responsible for the animations.

We'd all write for a couple of weeks, then meet up and read the material to each other and mark it. It was a bit like being at school, really. If everybody laughed at the sketch, then it got three asterisks. If it got a reasonable amount of laughs, but not total apoplexy, then it would get two. It got one if there were a few titters in it, and if it got no laughs at all, we'd try and sell it to someone else!

Usually David Frost.

Or else we'd try and reassign it—if it had some good things in it but wasn't quite tip-top, someone would usually say, "I'd like to have a go at that," and then they'd take it off and rewrite it.[1]

The five of us would often parody each other's writing styles, as well. For instance, the odd combination of Eric Idle and myself teamed up very early on to write a sketch (not a particularly good item, I don't think) that was a deliberate and very crude send-up of a typical Palin/Jones sketch of that time.[2] It was all shot on film and involved a man—a city stockbroker—who is so self-involved that he misses all the amazing events that are going on around him. It was very typical of their type of stuff at that time. Eric and I wrote it for just that reason, to see whether or not Mike and Terry would notice it at a script meeting and go "Aha!" But it got accepted.

Is "Pythonesque" a word? If it's not, it should be.

I don't feel that there was ever a conscious attempt within the group to write "Pythonesque." It was merely a curious thing that just happened when all six of us were together. A sort of

---

[1] Such was also the case with "Monty Python" episode #34, subtitled "The Cycling Tour." It began life as a non-"Python" Palin/Jones short script, which Cleese and Chapman took over, rewrote the final third, and turned into a "Python" episode.

[2] "The Extremely Dull Life of a City Stockbroker," episode #6.

odd blend that came out. I think that if any of us had gone off and deliberately tried to write a "Python" episode, it might have been quite close, but it wouldn't have had the quirky feeling you got because we were often cramming in material that didn't necessarily "fit."

If, for instance, John and I had written the majority of one episode and the others had no material in it at all, we'd feel guilty and try to crowd a bit of theirs in. As they would often do for us. It was always a process of rewriting.

Regardless, the only important factor overall was whether or not what we wrote amused the other people in the group. We weren't really too concerned whether the audience understood it. It all got down to voting around a table as to whether a piece of material should be in or out. And we always had, as a sort of secret weapon, the writer's veto. That is, if any one person within the group ever said, "No, that's going a bit far," then we would listen to that and the sketch would be out.

We were such good little boys. *Really*, we were!

As outrageous as the "Python" TV show was—and we were quite outrageous at times—we used to actually self-censor quite a lot. We were quite responsible people. Although there was *one* sketch I remember writing with John Cleese which we actually felt guilty about *while we were writing it*. Consequently, we laughed hysterically from beginning to end.

The sketch concerned a gentleman who had a little problem—his mother had recently died and he was wondering how to dispose of her. So he goes along with his mother in a sack (we're giggling already) to an undertaker's establishment and is advised by the undertaker that there are three things that he could do with his mother: She could be burnt, buried, or dumped.

Being burnt means (he explained) being put into the flames—*crackle crackle crackle*—which is not too nice, particularly if she's not quite dead. Being buried means being stuffed into the ground and eaten up by lots of worms and weevils—*nibble nibble nibble nibble*—which is also not too pleasant for the departed, especially if she's not quite dead. The third possibility was being dumped—thrown into the Thames or some such.

The man didn't regard any of the three as being really dignified enough for his mother, so the undertaker then came up with a *fourth* possibility—they could *eat* her. (John and I are laughing hysterically.) Now the man isn't too keen on this notion, but the undertaker encourages him, "She'd be delicious with a few French fries and broccoli!" Eventually the man says, "Well, I *am* a bit peckish. But no-no..." Then the undertaker says, "Look, I'll tell you what, we can eat your mom. Then, if you feel guilty about it, we can dig a grave and you can throw up into it."

By then we *had* gone too far.

The BBC evidently thought so, too, and wouldn't allow us to perform the sketch *unless we were attacked by the audience at the end of it*. Making it clear, one supposes, that we obviously had to be punished for such a gruesome sketch. So we rather artificially had to arrange for the audience to attack us at the end of the sketch, which was a mystifying moment. (If you look at the video of the sketch, Eric Idle appears to be anxious because of the audience's scattered boos. In reality, his concern was that the audience *wouldn't react properly and attack us*, as they were supposed to, and, therefore, we wouldn't be allowed to include the sketch in the show! What a silly situation to be in.)

This was the only time I remember that our veto system was tested. While we all thought it was funny, Terry Jones did express some initial concern in that he had an aging mother, but then we all had that same sort of queasiness about it—we were all laughing out of guilt. Nevertheless, we *did* shoot the sketch.

The word "wastebasket" was unknown to us

Truth be told, "Python" never was one to waste material, a fact borne out by the reuse of a lot of abandoned material from the first draft of our film, *Monty Python and the Holy Grail*, which we used in the fourth and final series of "Monty Python" (the last six episodes). There's one whole show that consisted mainly of material written by John and myself which wasn't used in *Holy Grail*. I compiled it, added to it, and basically pulled that episode together, with some help from Michael Palin and a little bit from Neil Innes.[3]

Interestingly, the *Holy Grail* film was originally going to take place in two different centuries. There was going to be the medieval story and also a modern-day section. In fact, in the modern version, we were going to have King Arthur discover the Holy Grail at the Grail counter in Harrod's department store,

---

3   The episode is subtitled, "Michael Ellis" and is show #42.

and it was going to end with God driving the getaway car! But we gradually fell more and more in love with the medieval stuff, with the atmosphere that we'd created, so most of the modern stuff disappeared—except for the historian and the policemen who came along, a device we used to end the movie.[4] Why end the movie that way? We simply couldn't afford a final battle scene.

Economy was also the reason coconuts were used instead of horses. We only had five and a half weeks or so to shoot the entire movie. If we'd had real horses, it would have taken at least 10 and a half, so we avoided the problem entirely by being creative and making something of it.

Common belief has it that, of the Pythons, it was mainly Michael Palin and Terry Jones who were concerned about the show's shape and structure, whereas John and myself were only concerned about things being funny. This is not true. The ant episode is a prime example of a show written mainly by John and myself. John had written some sketches with me, which were set in a department store, and I then put them into an order, rewrote them, and gave them Pythonic shape. Mike and Terry didn't even enter into it. While John certainly wanted everything to be as funny as it could be—he was very nit-picky about that, quite rightly—and while he was *not* too keen on things being visually splendid, it's wrong to say that only Mike and Terry were interested in the shape and structure of the shows. Yes they were, but they weren't the only ones.

---

4 Most of this aborted material can also be found in written form in the published script of the movie.

Of pepperpots, pet conversions, and the fish slapping dance

Much has been made of the apparent "intellectualism" of "Monty Python." Well, we're certainly not a dumb bunch—I mean we've got a historian (Terry Jones), a "word addict" (Idle), a lawyer (Cleese) and a medical doctor (me), but I don't think there's a great deal of depth behind the intellectual content of something like "The All-England Summarize Proust" sketch. I mean, obviously we had *heard* of the "big" literary and philosopher names and knew some rudimentary stuff about them, but certainly the person(s) who wrote that sketch didn't know everything that Proust had written or said. They probably knew enough to be able to get an O-level pass or work his name in a crossword.

What we quite liked was the juxtaposition, something that is exemplified in those mad female creatures that we played called *Pepperpots*—I hesitate to call them women.[5] Normally, they would be the last sort of people you'd expect to talk about philosophers, and yet they were always quite comfortable talking about Jean-Paul Sartre. That's where a lot of our humor came from, I think—the way that intellectual things were treated in a trivial way. I also think that a lot of our style is due to the fact that we were all other things in addition to being writers and actors.

---

5 "Pepperpots" was the code word the Pythons used to describe themselves when they played in drag—so named because their overall shape resembled a pepperpot.

Other times, sketches were written as a means to put people off. Such is the case with the "Pet Conversion" sketch.[6] The BBC had asked us to write a sort of quick, 10-minute section they could include in some Christmas show. We didn't want to do it, so we wrote something so unpleasant that they couldn't use it! That was the only reason that sketch was written, although we did later include it in a "Python" episode. Probably out of desperation for material.

We would also delight in the purely silly, sketches such as "The Fish Slapping Dance"—one of my favorite bits—or "The Batley Townswomen's Guild Presents the Battle of Pearl Harbor," which Eric was responsible for.

Nearly everything, however silly, was scripted, including one small sketch that appeared to be ad-libbed, but was, in fact, scripted—by me.[7] It was a small part, but one that I wanted to play, and I was rather annoyed when John whipped it off me.

Of course, there was no definite system at all when it came to parts. It didn't automatically follow that the person who wrote the sketch also got the role. It usually came down to whoever had the balls to say, "I want to do this," which usually wasn't me as I was more interested in going off to the bar and

---

6 "Pet Conversion" (episode #10) is a Chapman/Cleese sketch that involves John as a customer who wants to buy a cat. Michael Palin is the pet shop owner who seems to be right out of cats, though he does have a terrier and spends the remainder of the sketch describing the many vile ways that you can turn a terrier into a cat, a bird, and a fish.

7 The sketch—"Policeman ('Come back to my place')," episode #13—involves a man who complains to a policeman that his wallet had been stolen. The policeman questions the man for a few moments, without any luck, and then the man says, "Do you want to come back to my place?" to which the policeman replies, "Yeah, all right."

having a drink. But it *did* mean that I sometimes didn't get the credit, as a writer, for a sketch that I had co-authored, such as "The Parrot Sketch," which John and I wrote and John and Mike played. Generally speaking, though, with John and myself being the tallest, most of the authority roles went to us, leaving all the mad, short-people roles to the others!

CHAPTER 5

Paralyzed at the Polo Lounge

There were a lot of outrageous things that tended to happen to me in those sort of hazy, alcohol days...

I remember once that I went to the Polo Lounge in the Beverly Hills Hotel. I don't quite remember *why*, but I do remember looking about me at all the opulence and deciding that the people in the Polo Lounge didn't care all that much about less fortunate people in the world. I don't know *how* I got that feeling.

Anyway, this got to me in my drunken state, and I decided that I had to do something to irritate these people. But what? Well, I felt that making them as uncomfortable as possible was a good start, so I decided then and there to pretend to be paralyzed from the waist down.

A pox on waiters who don't get the joke

After a moment to get my bearings, I let out a sudden shriek and began to thrash about the table, sending all manner of expensive dishes and glasses crashing to the floor. This, of course, caused everyone in the restaurant to stop what they were doing and look at me. It also immediately brought the waiter. I informed him that I needed a wheelchair at once as I'd suddenly become paralyzed. He didn't believe me, of course, because he'd seen me walk in, but I told him, "Yes, this *is* a joke, but I'm playing it to the hilt! I'm not going to move from the waist down from this point on, so would you get me a wheelchair?"

He was somewhat reluctant to oblige me, but by now everyone in the Polo Lounge was staring at him, and even his manager had come to the table to see what was the matter. He explained to his manager that I was a comedian (he'd evidently recognized me) and that I didn't really *need* a wheelchair; in fact, it was all a joke. The manager asked me if this was true, and I said, "Yes, but I am still a patron of this restaurant, and I demand a wheelchair!"

After a few moments of heated discussion, the manager told the waiter to fetch the wheelchair and wheel me out of the Beverly Hills Hotel. Now the waiter was, I think, rather annoyed. He thought I was up to something (obviously), and we didn't get quite as far as my limo before he stopped and said that he wasn't going to go any further with this "joke." So he turned and left, leaving me in the lobby in this chair.

And on the people who leave them tips

Fortunately for me, there also happened to be a fund-raiser for some political organization going on at the hotel, and a lot of Very Important People were just arriving. "Well," I thought, "if that's the waiter's attitude, then I will take this through to its extremity." So I waited for the bulk of the crowd to enter and then, shrieking loudly, I threw myself to the ground and (to the horror of the VIPs) began to crawl, hand over hand, into the back of my limo.

I don't think my little joke did much for the reputation of the waiter or the Beverly Hills Hotel.

At least I certainly hope not.

CHAPTER 6

Other dangerous liaisons (and more on the inestimable Mr. Cleese)

There were no hard and fast rules regarding writing partnerships in "Python." I've written with lots of people in the past. I even wrote little bits with Michael Palin when John left the series, and a little bit with Douglas Adams.

Douglas is a man whom many of you know as the creator of the immensely successful series of books called The Hitchhiker's Guide to the Galaxy. I wrote one sketch with Douglas, which was used on "Python," concerning a doctor who refuses to treat a patient who is quite blatantly gushing blood until he answers lots of irritating questions about motor racing. (Not that that sort of thing *ever* goes on in the medical profession, I can *assure* you!) Douglas Adams later collaborated on many projects that never saw the light of day, including "Our Show for Ringo Starr" (see Chapter 10 for "the light of day") and "Out of the Trees" (which did have one, unannounced airing and then promptly disappeared from sight). He also co-wrote a sketch about Marilyn Monroe, which eventually ended up in a rewritten state on the *Monty Python and the Holy Grail* soundtrack.

Neil Innes, late of the fabulous Bonzo Dog Doo-Dah Band, was also a sort of "seventh mad musical Python," and, while he was not involved in the television series very much, he contributed musically to *Holy Grail*, along with Eric Idle, and was further involved with Eric in the Rutles.

The songs in Monty Python were most particularly Eric's province. For instance, he wrote "Look on the Bright Side" for *Life of Brian*, and "The Penis Song" for *Meaning of Life*. Though there were exceptions—"The Lumberjack Song" was Michael Palin and Terry Jones, and "Bing Tiddle Tiddle Bong" was written by myself and Fred Tomlinson—more often than not you'd be fairly safe on betting that, if there's a song there, then it was Eric's.

Actually, I think Eric always rather wanted to be a pop star, and that's quite possibly why he'd frequently be seen hanging around people like Mick Jagger and so on. In fact, it was his friendship with Mick that led to his appearing in Jamaica at one point, while we were there writing *Life of Brian*. It was an *extraordinary* evening in that we were in this isolated house and we finished up with nothing better to do than to play charades, which is really rather strange. It was particularly memorable, though, because Mick Jagger was given as his subject, the movie, *Shaft in Africa*. I must say that his portrayal of that movie on the floor was really quite...graphic. A very memorable moment, indeed.

How silly talks turned into silly walks

As you should know by now (you *have* been paying attention, haven't you?), I did most of my writing with John Cleese. Our habit was to work together either out of my house or his. I'd usually arrive about 10 o'clock in the morning (although I was always about half an hour late, even when we met at my own house), and we'd break around lunch time. The mornings usually started with some preliminary chit-chat and then we'd start working. Actually, we'd start *thinking* about starting to *think* about working. All right, I suppose we were both trying to *avoid* working, as we'd sit there and drink endless cups of coffee, chat about the news, do the crosswords, read the newspapers— *anything* to put off that truly awful moment of *actually having to write something funny down on paper.*

Sometimes during the course of that hour and a half or so of doing almost nothing, an idea would finally emerge that would lead us on to a sketch, and our day's work would be done.

But it didn't always work out that way. I remember one particular morning when nothing had really sallied forth, so we resorted to our final tactic, which was to open up *Roget's Thesaurus* and merely stare at words. This would sometimes spark ideas—the whole of the "Cheese Shop Sketch" came straight out of *Roget's Thesaurus*. And I'm very grateful for it, too.

Anyway, on this particular day, John and myself were stuck and had resorted to *Roget's* and were just staring at words. Suddenly we noticed that the word we were staring at was "anger." Anger anger anger... We *felt* anger. We *thought* anger. We *drank* anger.

And still we dawdled. What should we *write* about anger? John was quite keen on doing *something* with it, as anger is an emotion he portrays particularly well, but after several attempts we reluctantly decided that we couldn't really see *what* to do with anger. So, now what?

We happened to have been talking that morning about a minister in the government—the Wilson government in Britain—who'd just been appointed to cabinet rank. He appeared to all and sundry to be a man who clearly had *no* abilities at all. At the time, he hadn't actually been designated as Minister *for* anything, certainly not for anything responsible like Minister of Housing or the Foreign Ministry, so he hadn't yet received a title. But, fortunately for this man, the country then went for about two or three weeks without any rain and he subsequently became Minister for Drought (that was the first time we'd ever had one of *those*!). Well, it wasn't that important a job—in fact, there wasn't actually much to do at all in the position—but since the man was completely incompetent, it seemed like a reasonable sort of job to give him.

But then it so happened that he was very *successful* in this ministry because, of course, it *rained*. In fact, it rained so much that he subsequently became Minister for Flooding! I realize that that sounds absolutely stupid, but it's quite true. Anyway, this incident gave us the idea for some sort of *silly* ministry. "Ministry of Anger?" we thought. "The Ministry of Anger...how could that go? No-no-no, that didn't really lead anywhere."

Now, on this particular day, John and I were working out of my house, which stood on a hill. As we sat there trying to decide what we could or could not write about the Ministry of Anger, I happened to glance out of my window and noticed a gentleman walking past and up the hill. I immediately recognized him as being the same gentleman that I'd seen walk past my house and up the hill the week before, and I remembered him because this gentleman had a very strange ability—he was somehow able to walk uphill *while leaning backwards!*

It was the most extraordinary angle. I don't know *how* he managed to do it, I mean, I actually ran outside to try and get a glimpse of the footwork, but by the time I'd got outside, he'd disappeared. But I came back in with a notion: "Ah! *Silly walks!*"

So, "The Ministry of Silly Walks" it was. But, by now it was very nearly lunch time, so we rang up Michael Palin and Terry Jones and *they* wrote the sketch.

The day Eric killed John

Believe it or not, we didn't really have many complaints about the "Python" television series, but I do remember one in particular because it concerned myself. It was written by a very angry lady from Newcastle, England. The rage in her heart literally dripped from every word. Her complaint concerned an appearance I'd made on a talk show in England hosted by a gentleman called George Melly.

Now George Melly is an English jazz singer.[1] A very *good* jazz singer, actually. He's a full Renaissance man, as he's also an expert in fine arts, a very good author, and general *bon vivant*. His notion for this talk show was that he should only invite people whom he knew. Not only so he wouldn't have to do a whole load of research, but also so he wouldn't have to have a clipboard full of notes or anything and he could just have a very casual conversation with his guests and, hopefully, bring the best out of them.

In order to ensure such a conclusion, the hospitality before these shows was of *formidable* proportions. There were incredible quantities of alcohol freely available, and other things, too.[2]

Anyway, this meant that I appeared on his show in a *very* relaxed frame of mind.

Just before I went on, George had been talking about a book he'd written called *Owning Up*, in which he'd admitted

---

[1] If that's not a contradiction in terms.
[2] Of course, because he *was* a musician.

indulging in "certain intimate practices" while he was a member of Her Majesty's Navy. Not that that sort of thing happens in the British Navy AND IT NEVER WILL!!! (And neither does cannibalism...) So I went on the show in this very relaxed mood and admitted that I, myself, had taken part in similar activities in my past. That was the substance of this lady's complaint. She wrote to the Python office (we had one by then), saying that:

> **"Someone from "Monty Python" who hadn't had the courage to give his name..."**

Well, that was monstrous really because obviously George had introduced me as Graham Chapman and had spoken to me as Graham throughout, and there at the end of the program it said: TALKING TO GEORGE MELLY WAS GRAHAM CHAPMAN... well, never mind, anyway...

> **"was evidently homosexual and therefore deserved eternal hellfire and damnation."**

And it went on in similar fire-and-brimstone rhetoric for about two-and-a-half pages. She'd also included 25 sheets of paper on which she'd written various prayers which "if this person said everyday for the rest of his life, he might obtain some kind of purgatory."

That was her best offer.

Eric Idle had a wonderful idea—he wrote back to her saying, "We've found out which one of us it was...and we killed him!"

It's interesting to note that the next six programs we did, the last six programs we *ever* did, were the ones without John Cleese in them. I'm not sure *what* she made of that.[3]

And I don't care.

---

[3] I think, in retrospect, that it was a good idea to have stopped when we did, leaving 45 half-hour shows as the total number. We then felt, as John had a season earlier, that while we probably could have gone on and done more and they probably would have been as good, what was the point? Those last six episodes of "Python" were rather unique in that, by that time, we had created our own little world. We had begun to think of shows as a whole rather than a series of sketches. We were consciously trying to get more of a shape into a show, with an eye toward movies, I suppose, which, of course, followed.

CHAPTER 7

Genital exposure is no problem. I am, after all, a doctor

After the success of *Monty Python and the Holy Grail*, we all went to Paris for a day (to see what we all sounded like in French, I suppose) and chatted about what the next movie would be about. We thought perhaps they could find the Grail and we could take it from there.

But then Eric Idle came up with a monstrous suggestion—a title for the next movie:

Jesus Christ—Lust for Glory!

Of course, we couldn't possible *do* that, but it did give us the thought that something set in that period, in the time of

Christ, would be a very good area for us to work in. Particularly as we'd done most of the research—I mean, we'd all read the Bible. Our initial thought was something like *The Gospel According to St. Brian*, and Brian was going to be a "thirteenth apostle" who was always late turning up for miracles. That sort of thing.

The reason we wanted to write the movie was because we felt that churches had rather missed the central point of Christ's arguments, which were that people should love one another. Instead, they got rather diverted into joining separate little clubs, wearing different clothing and thinking of themselves as being "rather special," and those other people over there as being "*not* rather special," and therefore not worthy of going to heaven. Call us wrong, but we felt that this wasn't very Christian of them.

As usual, it fell to John Cleese and myself to write some of the opening material for this movie, and we clearly thought at that time that we ought to write a Nativity scene. However, we couldn't quite see how to write a Nativity scene because that would obviously involve Mr. Christ, with whom we had absolutely no quarrel at all. I mean, he was a pretty nice person. He didn't put many fingers wrong at all, we didn't think. We generally agreed with his teachings and felt he was a very good person indeed.[1] The man was absolutely irreproachable. So no problem with him or his teachings. Wonderful bloke. Wonderful, wonderful...

---

[1] Oh, he got a bit tetchy once and caused a fig tree or an olive bush to be withered or something, but that was only a little fit of pique. Anyone can have an off day. But otherwise, he was perfect!

Our solution to avoiding Christ was to write a Nativity scene that had the Three Wise Men clearly going to the wrong manger—Brian's manger. However, this did not stop the bigots from complaining, and, consequentially, *Life of Brian* turned out to be a very successful venture.[2] (It is interesting to note that these various church organizations all felt quite comfortable complaining about the movie without ever having seen it. But then, that's the prerogative of a bigot, isn't it?)

I recall one moment of *amazing* embarrassment which occurred during the filming of *Life of Brian*. We filmed in Tunisia which is, of course, in North Africa, where most people happen to be Muslim people, Mohammedan folks. On this particular occasion, I'd just spent the whole day (as Brian) being chased by a load of followers I had no wish to have. I eventually manage to escape them and then spent my very first night with my newly acquired girlfriend, Judith Iscariot.

Well, I'd had a wonderful night and wake up the next morning, full of "the Joys of Spring"—and totally naked. So, in the scene, I throw open the shutters, only to discover this huge band of followers waiting outside for me.

Let me say here that the matter of genital exposure is no particular problem to me—I am a doctor after all—but there *was* a problem in that we had this crowd of Tunisian extras—some 300 people posing as 600—and half of that number were *women*. And Muslim women are forbidden by Muslim law to see such things. It's absolutely *forbidden* for them to even *think* of

---

[2] In a way it was very nice of them, as they did all of the publicity for us!

viewing naughty bits. So when I flung open the shutters, half the crowd ran away screaming!

That had a profound effect on my psyche. I'd like to think it was their religion... Yes, I'm sure that it was.

CHAPTER 8

When do you stop doing nothing?

It's not very often one gets invited to speak to the Cambridge/Oxford University Union. Thank God. Well, it's called a "union" but it's a debating chamber really, and one of its main functions seems to be for people to rehearse and be noticed as potential members of Parliament. It is very much a sort of "talking shop," and a rather pompous one at that, so therefore I didn't like the place very much at all. Anyway, one day I was invited to go and speak at the Union, and after some trepidation I decided to go, dressed as a carrot, where I proceeded to do and say absolutely nothing.

Now, "nothing" is a very interesting thing to do. I mean, for one thing, it's very difficult to *stop* doing nothing. For that matter, how does one really know when they've *started* doing nothing? I suppose that the carrot "not being there" and then the carrot "being there" meant I'd started doing nothing.

Anyway, there *was* one person there who knew my plan, whom I had told I wasn't going to speak—a rather odd poet called Ivor Cutler.[1] Ivor took his place beside me and proceeded to sit through all the speakers before me with his fingers lodged firmly in his ears. When I stood up—to say nothing, of course—he proceeded to "listen" in rapt attention.

Anyway, after about 10 minutes of my standing before the Union, dressed as a carrot and saying and doing absolutely nothing—watching the audience work its way from extreme embarrassment, to cat-calls, to laughter, back to embarrassment, back to laughter again—I was ready to get the hell out of there. I muttered something to that effect to Ivor, who promptly stood up and read out an absurd poem, which I think he may have made up on the spur of the moment. It didn't make any sense to me, and I'm certain it didn't make any sense to the Union, but it did give me an opportunity to leave the room.

Which I did. At which point, I guess, I officially stopped doing nothing.

The most amazing thing is, the Union still occasionally asks me back to speak.

I just never bother to reply.

---

[1] Perhaps best known to Beatle fans as Buster Bloodvessel in their *Magical Mystery Tour* film.

CHAPTER 9

A bunch of Pythons could occasionally turn into a nest of vipers

As close as I think we all are to each other, it would be a grave error on my part (if not an outright lie) if I didn't touch upon the fact that there were times when there were differences of opinion among our stalwart troupe. Emotions *did* sometimes run high, particularly between the two extremes of the group— the very cold and logical John Cleese, and the very emotional Terry Jones. Both, at times, were equally at fault for incidences of unpleasantness.

John would often goad Terry, purposely, into situations of rage, quickly getting Terry to the point where all he could emit was a high-pitched Welsh whine.

Terry was equally at fault for being so persistent in his views and so unwilling to listen to argument, just *knowing* passionately in his guts that something was right, and refusing absolutely to admit that he could *possibly* be wrong.

So those two extremes naturally led to a few *fiery* moments. But only once to actual physical violence. That was when an ashtray was thrown by one at the other during discussions on whether or not a certain piece of material should be included in *Holy Grail.*

Said ashtray missed its intended target.

Looking on the bright side of Eric Idle

I suppose that *my* parallel within the group would have to be Eric Idle, although I'm not quite certain what we're the poles *of*, as we think alike on many issues. Perhaps we're an east/west pole. I think that we approach the same things differently. I think Eric expects people to be devious, where I expect them to be straightforward. I'm stupidly trusting, and Eric's unduly suspicious. That sort of thing.

This hasn't led to any particular antagonisms, except perhaps on the business side of things. Creatively, Eric and I have written together quite well, although on the whole Eric is more of a loner. John is also quite a loner, although not in terms of writing. Eric is very protective of what he's created, and he will stick by that, come what may. He finds it very difficult to partake in the "give-and-take" that you have to have in a writing relationship.

That's another way that Eric and I differ, in that I very much *like* collaborating, having another mind there to work with and react to. To embellish and improve upon, I suppose. Of course, Eric had a very difficult time of it in "Monty Python" in that he *was* on his own. Each one of us had an ally—John had me, Mike had Terry, and then there was Eric on his own. I wouldn't have liked to be in that position. I wouldn't have had the *guts* to be in that position, as Python could be the *worst* audience in the world! We would sometimes withhold laughs out of jealousy or spite or just sheer bad manners. But I think that all of us, fortunately, were usually able to subjugate any personal feelings (and personal hurts) because the end result was something that was created by "Python the group" more than by a group of individuals. There was a group "mind-think," if you will, a corporate-consciousness and communal spirit.

Painting a picture of Terry Gilliam

Terry Gilliam was a whole other department altogether. He did his animations and came to group meetings where material was read aloud, but where he was very useful was whenever there were group disputes. Often there would be a situation in which there were two people who felt very strongly *against* something, two who felt very strongly *for* it, and one undecided—so Terry would swing the balance.

It was good to have a like-minded outsider—and I say "outsider" because he *had* to be separate, really. The nature of his work was so intricate and involved that it took nearly every moment of every waking day for him to get the material together for each series. Terry never contributed much to the sketches, as the written word was not really his domain.

John often used to rib him—well, we all did I suppose—about his use of the English language in that it was, well, *limited*. In fact, John claimed that Terry's vocabulary *stretched* to only about 30 words. John used to say that things with Terry would either be "really great" or they would "really piss him off." Not many shades of meaning in between that.

I especially remember one occasion when we were doing a stage tour of Canada and were flying over Lake Superior, and Terry looked down, turned around to the rest of us and said, "Hey, look, you guys, a whole bunch of water!"

While Terry is very good visually—*extremely* good visually—as evidenced by his excellent direction of several wonderful movies, clearly the word department is *not* his *metier*.

They like me! They really like me!

I think that the most interesting moment, as far as group spirit is concerned, came after we finished filming *Life of Brian*. While we were filming the movie, a very nice film critic named Ian Johnson was making a documentary, one of those "The Making of..." things. Now, while we did have a kind of control over this documentary, in that we had approval and could stop it from being shown, we wanted to give Ian his artistic head and try to keep things as he wanted, mainly because we wanted it to be a reasonably realistic view of things.

When the time came for us all to view this documentary, I think we all went along with some trepidation. I suspect we were all a bit whanged, worried about what would turn up on screen, as we were all *very* conscious of the fact that each of us had been asked by Ian how we felt about the other members of the group and we had no idea what was going to end up being in the final 50-minute piece. Of course, I went in there knowing what *I'd* said about all of *them* and was thinking, "Well, they would have all had the same opportunity to say what they felt about *me*, so what *is* this afternoon going to be like? It's going to be a bit awkward!"

Well, it wasn't *too* bad, though I do think we'd all been more honest about each other than we'd ever been before, even if it was done in a light spirit, with a kind of "jokey" air about it. At the end of the film, there was that one moment where we all sort of looked at each other, and I think all of us understood the same truth at the same time: "Yes, I know you. I know your good points, your bad points, but, the hell with all that anyway, because—I like you."

That was a very *nice* moment, and I think it is a feeling that will always be there.

PART TWO

Silly Bits

CHAPTER 10

"It's"

The Ringo Starr Show

Of all the scripts that I have written, aside from my work on "Python," there is this one that seems to have taken on a life of its own. It has become legendary, and I don't quite know why. Perhaps it's because it involved a Beatle. Perhaps it's because it never got beyond the scripting stage, so no one's ever seen it. I don't know—you tell me.

"It" is a script I co-wrote with Douglas Adams, for a proposed series called "Our Show for Ringo Starr." It's Michael Palin who is partly responsible for its creation. In fact, "It's" is the reason for its creation at all.

Perhaps I should explain. Michael Palin created a character we used during "Python's" first season, one whom we dubbed the "It's" Man—a shabbily-dressed, hermit-like man who struggled across difficult terrain to get his sentence in on television. Unfortunately, he could never get beyond the word "It's..." before being interrupted by the opening titles. And it's the "It's" Man who is behind the creation of "Our Show for Ringo Starr." There. It's all pretty straightforward after that.

One day, we decided to give the "It's" Man an opportunity to do more, to finally speak his peace. So at the end of show #28, we had Michael, dressed as the "It's" Man, come out as host of his own chat show. He was finally going to be allowed to get out the rest of this important sentence, which had always been interrupted. Guests for this pretend chat show were going to basically include any famous people we could get, and as luck would have it, Ringo and Lulu obliged us to come along to the studio and "not be interviewed."[1] (John Cleese and I knew Ringo and had already worked with him on *The Magic Christian* film. Since we had all gotten along, it made perfect sense to invite him and that was probably why he decided to come along.)

Anyway, the joke was for the "It's" Man to come out to a big musical fanfare and then, when he finally got the opportunity to say what had been on his mind all these months, he got no further than "Hello, good evening, welcome. It's..." when the signature tune kicked in and the titles began, basically cutting him off. Again. It was all great fun, and Ringo and Lulu

---

[1] Actually, John and Yoko Lennon were first approached about being the guests on "It's." John, a big "Monty Python" fan, happily agreed, but they were involved in an automobile accident soon after and couldn't do it.

seemed to enjoy themselves. This gave us the idea to maybe try and work with Ringo again later on—which is how this whole story ties together and makes some sense. Doesn't it?

A few years later, Douglas Adams and I wrote a special for Ringo, a part science-fiction, part historical-fiction story that loosely revolved around a few of Ringo's hit songs.[2] It was never approved by any networks or by cable TV—I think they thought it a "bit rude" and, quite frankly, I don't think they understood it very much. It would have made a very nice show, though I highly doubt that it will ever be made now. But it has achieved a sort of legendary status and still crops up every now and then.

For those of you wondering what the hell I'm talking about, allow me to give you a snippet of the script, published here, I dare say, for the first time anywhere...and almost certainly for the last.

---

2 "Our Show for Ringo Starr" was loosely based around Ringo's "Goodnight, Vienna" and "Ringo" records. A sort of expanded music video, its story featured Ringo as the great, great, great, great-grandson of a prince (although that had absolutely nothing to do with the story) who works a mundane office job and becomes involved with an exact double named Rinog Trars, who lives in an alternative universe. There are robots and spaceships and lots of troubles with narrators. In style, it owes more to Douglas Adams and his later *Hitchhiker* books than to Graham. Sections of the script involving a spaceship called the B-ark were later excised and used by Douglas in his book, *The Restaurant at the End of the Universe*.

GRAHAM Crackers

An excerpt from
Our Show for Ringo Starr

By Nemona Lethbridge and Vera Hunt
(a.k.a. Graham Chapman & Douglas Adams)
©1987 Seagoat Productions, Ltd.

15 to 30 Seconds—Opening Credits

"I'm the Greatest"

Ringo in *Goodnight, Vienna* costume, neutral setting, pointing, like God, at things as we see them happen, including:

- Rocket launching.
- Atom bomb exploding.
- The summit of Mt. Everest.
- Spanish hotel blowing up and down (film and reverse film) with accompanying accordian music.
- New York being flattened by enormous mouse dropping on it.
- Knockout blow from Mohammed Ali.
- Chairman Mao.
- Enormous crowds cheering wildly.
- Paramilitary police shooting up bed of roses.
- Person in ant costume having cup of tea. He is messily crushed by an enormous boot—cod fairy tale music.

Throughout the following we see shots of typical happy fairy tale-type rustic villagers, princes, knights, Little Bo Peeps, dragons, etc. During narration, all these characters become aware that the narrator isn't talking about them and stand looking at camera, bemused that their stories are not being taken up.

Narrator

Once upon a time, a long time ago, ooh, it must have been, ooh, ages—so long ago I can't remember it, and my friend, Godfrey, who's 37, *he* can't remember it, so it must have been a *long* time ago. I mean, come on, I'm not talking about measly little bits of time, minutes and all that, but proper grown-up years and I mean *lots* of them. Anyway, a long time ago in a far, far land, I mean a *really* long way, I mean you may think it's a long way down the road to the hardware store, but that's just peanuts to *this* sort of distance, there lived a handsome prince. Well, not *particularly* handsome in fact, though *bits* of him were handsome, I mean where do you draw the line, I mean some people find long flowing blond hair and a retrousse nose very handsome. I mean, I don't personally, but then all opinions are subjective. If I had to, I'd say that I prefer the sort who's dark, stocky, and good at math.

Action occurs as Narrator speaks (voice over).

Narrator

Anyway, this prince, whom some people probably found attractive, was out walking in the woods one

81

day, when he fell off a cliff and died very messily,
which prevented him from living happily ever after.

Stunned looks on the faces of all the characters.

Narrator
But his great, great, great, great, great-grandson
worked in an office.

Cut to Office.

Fairy Tale Characters V/O
What? What about us?

Enter Director.

Director V/O
Sorry, loves, that's all.

Fairy Tale Characters V/O
What? It took me hours to get into this costume.

Director V/O
Well, that's all there is.

Fairy Tale Characters V/O
Look, can't we be in one more shot?

Director V/O
All right, all right.

**Three-second shot of fairy tale characters waving at
camera, then cut back to office.**

Fairy Tale Characters V/O

Well, that wasn't much better—do we still get the whole fee?

In office, Ringo is standing, leaning against desk.

Ringo

Have you done now—can we get on with it?

Narrator

Well...

Camera begins to stray away.

Narrator

Ah, yes.

Camera jumps back.

Ringo

Well, I'm glad to hear that. I've been hanging around here for hours.

Narrator

Anyway this person who was extremely boring and uninteresting worked in this dull drab office. It's impossible to say how appallingly dull and boring it all was.

Ringo

Look, just leave it to me, will you?

Narrator

What!?

Ringo

Push off!

Narrator

Well, I haven't finished yet.

Ringo

Yes, you have, you are not needed.

Narrator

Do I still get a full fee?

Ringo

Shut up. Now at last I can get on with it.

He stands against wall and holds two handles. Wall section pivots backwards like thunder birds and Ringo goes down a chute, muttering "bloody narrators."

Narrator

I heard that.

Ringo

Good!

CHAPTER 11

Pythonesque sketches you've never seen...or heard... or thought of... or wondered about

The following three sketches were written by Graham Chapman and Jim Yoakum in the year before Graham's death.

According to Yoakum, "This was a (rather mundane) sketch of mine that Graham proceeded to take into outer space with the absurd suggestions that the beggar and his family consisted on plankton and that, while the beggar was not a mute, he was 'rather quiet.'"

The Charity Case

A street. A Beggar approaches a City Gent waiting for the bus.

Beggar

Excuse me, sir...

City Gent

Yes, hello?

The Beggar hands the City Gent a small card.

City Gent

Reading.

"I am a deaf mute selling this card to support my family. We are so poor we must eat plankton and small spores. Please contribute 1 pound, thank you."

To Beggar.

Is this yours?

Beggar

Yes sir. May I have a contribution?

City Gent

But this card says that you're a deaf mute.

Beggar

So?

City Gent

So you're not.

Beggar

Yes, I am.

City Gent

If you're a deaf mute then how do you know what I'm saying?

Beggar

Cups hand to ear, pretending to be deaf.

Excuse me?

City Gent

Oh don't pull that "excuse me" business! You understood perfectly well what I said.

Beggar

Er, I can read minds.

City Gent

I don't believe it. You must read lips.

Beggar

No, minds. Look I can prove it...

He covers his eyes with his hand.

87

Beggar

Now you say something to me.

City Gent

Testing one, two, three. Testing.

Beggar

Repeating back.

Testing one, two, three. Testing. See?

City Gent

That's amazing. But how is it that you can talk?

Beggar

Yes, well, you've got me there, sir.

City Gent

Aha! You're *not* really a mute.

Beggar

No, sir. And I'm not really deaf, either.

City Gent

Thrown.

You're not!?

Beggar

To tell you the truth, sir, I'm selling these cards for my brother who really *is* a deaf mute.

City Gent

Why can't your brother sell them himself?

Beggar

He's at his viola class today.

City Gent

Yes, well, I don't believe you.

Beggar

Too bad. Can I have the pound anyway?

City Gent

I'm not going to give you any money. Please go away.

Beggar

Oh, come on, it's only a pound!

City Gent

No, you lied to me. It's the principle.

Beggar

But my family has to eat coal dust to survive! We're so poor we have to live in a hole in the road!

City Gent

I'm sorry.

Beggar

To be honest, sir, I *do* have a bit of a lump in one ear, and I have a tendency to be rather quiet.

City Gent

That's hardly equal to being a deaf mute.

Beggar

Then just give me seventy-five pence.

City Gent

I'll give you ten to leave me alone.

Beggar

What?! Those cards *cost* me twenty!

City Gent

It's my final offer.

Beggar

Oh... all right.

The City Gent hands him ten pence. The Beggar starts to walk off, then stops.

Beggar

How much for a game leg?

City Gent

Are you lame? Really?

Beggar

Well, the left is a bit stiff.

City Gent

Five pence.

Beggar

Done!

The City Gent hands the Beggar five pence and gets on his bus.

Beggar

Counting his money.

Ha! There's one born every minute.

"More Room in the Amoire" is a stream-of-consciousness thing that came about while Graham was describing to Jim Yoakum a sketch he and John Cleese had written for "Monty Python" about two Pepperpot women discussing why a penguin was on top of their television set. While he was describing the sketch, Graham began using the Pepperpot voice and making up these mad things (including the first four or five lines that kicked this off) and it went on (and on) from there.

More Room in the Armoire

A sitting room. Two pepperpotty women, Mrs. Anaplasty and Mrs. Short-Five-P-for-the-Post, are chatting while an inane radio program drones on in the background.

Mrs. Short-Five-P-for-the-Post
And how did you sleep, last night, dear?

Mrs. Anaplasty
On my back, I think. Although I can't be sure. I slept through most of it. How about you?

Mrs. Short-Five-P-for-the-Post
Funny you should ask. The first stage went off all right, but I had a bit of bother during my R.E.M. phase, until I remembered my Mneumonic Induction for Lucid Dreams.

Mrs. Anaplasty
Polysomnograph hooked up?

Mrs. Short-Five-P-for-the-Post

I think so. Anyway, when I finally dropped off into full R.E.M. lucid dream phase, you know, complete left-right-left-right eye movement and all that, I discovered the most amazing thing.

Mrs. Anaplasty

What's that?

Mrs. Short-Five-P-for-the-Post

That I hate my father.

Mrs. Anaplasty

But we *all* hate your father.

Beat.

My uvula's acting up again. When I woke-up this morning there was margarine all over the bed.

Mrs. Short-Five-P-for-the-Post

That sounds serious. Perhaps you should see a doctor. I think that psychophysicologist is still living under the sink.

Mrs. Anaplasty

That quack? He gave Mrs. Red Chinese Threat rabies shots because she dreamed of fire hydrants. Is that nice parapsychologist still living under the stair?

93

Mrs. Short-Five-P-for-the-Post

Which one's that, dear?

Mrs. Anaplasty

Doctor Lepzig. The one with the fear of 12th-century German armor.

Mrs. Short-Five-P-for-the-Post

Oh no, he moved out ages ago! I believe he went to rid Africa of natty formal attire.

A man enters wearing a dressing gown. He climbs into a cabinet.

Mrs. Short-Five-P-for-the-Post

Good morning Your Highness!

To Mrs Anaplasty.

I know, Doctor LeBerge is still staying in the fridge. He should be able to help you.

They rise and go to the refrigerator, opening the door.

Mrs. Short-Five-P-for-the-Post

Yoo hoo! Doctor LeBerge?

Dr. LeBerge

Voice over.

Shut that bloody door! I'm nearly reaching a breakthrough!

The pepperpots shut the door.
SFX: Lascivious moans and grunts.

Mrs. Short-Five-P-for-the-Post

Ooh, he's gotten the big head, hasn't he?

Mrs. Anaplasty

Yes, he's not the man I married.

Mrs. Short-Five-P-for-the-Post

You *didn't* marry him, dear, you married that fellow what does voice-overs for the *National Geographic* specials.

Mrs. Anaplasty

Jack Palance?

Mrs. Short-Five-P-for-the-Post

No, not Jack Palance. Who's the fellow who *sounds* like Jack Palance but *isn't* Jack Palance?

Mrs. Anaplasty

Oh, you mean the one that does voice-overs for the National Geographics.

Mrs. Short-Five-P-for-the-Post

That's the one!

Mrs. Anaplasty

Oh yes, he's very nice. Lovely speaking voice.

Mrs. Short-Five-P-for-the-Post

Oh yes. Now he's what I'd call a *real* man. Very sexy.

Mrs. Anaplasty

Yes.

They giggle.

Mrs. Anaplasty

Beat.

Er, who's sexy, dear?

Mrs. Short-Five-P-for-the-Post

The man who does voice-overs for the *National Geographic.*

Mrs. Anaplasty

Jack Palance?

There is a knock on the door. Mrs. Anaplasty goes to answer it. A postman stands outside with a bundle of letters.

Postman

Morning, Mrs Anaplasty.

Mrs. Anaplasty

Hello. Are all these for me?

Postman

Yes, that'll be 75 pounds please. Plus VAT.

Mrs. Anaplasty

What? 75 pounds just for delivering the mail?

Postman

Well, now, that's hardly ordinary mail. You've got quite a nice bundle there—a couple of air mails, some third classers and a magazine. Quite diverse, actually.

Mrs. Anaplasty

There's hardly enough here to choke a rabbit.

Postman

Well, price is not based strictly on weight ratios. You've got some real top-hole reading material there. That postcard from Doctor Lepzig alone is worth at least 10 pounds, I should think. Came all the way from Africa.

Mrs. Anaplasty

So? *You* didn't trot it across the bloody Sahara.

Postman

That's hardly the point, is it? I mean, be fair, that stuff is twice as good as the rubbish you'd get from one of those overnight mail services.

Mrs. Anaplasty

Yes. But I'm still not giving you 75 quid for it.

Postman

Oh all right. How about giving me "a little" then?

He makes a grope for her. She shrieks and pushes him out the door.

Mrs. Short-Five-P-for-the-Post

It's hell to pay when they don't get their rate hikes.

A man in a scuba outfit walks past.

Mrs. Short-Five-P-for-the-Post

Hello, Mr Cousteau! I'm afraid that Zsa-Zsa Gabor is using the bath this morning, but you can go diving in the loo, if you'd like.

Cousteau

Exiting.

Zoot allures!

SFX: A loud splash.

Cousteau

Voice over.

Non! Non!

98

SFX: A loud flushing.

Mrs. Anaplasty

Oh, dear. Zsa-Zsa's flushed Jacques down the loo.

Mrs. Short-Five-P-for-the-Post

Oh well, it leaves more room in the armoire.

This was one of the first things Graham and Jim Yoakum ever collaborated on. Yoakum remembers, "We had no real idea what we were going to do with the finished product, probably nothing, but it served its purpose—to see if we could create together. The sketch came to life after he started telling me of a rather frustrating experience he'd had with a bank that had refused to perform some very perfunctory service. I think the whole sketch adequately sums up his feelings towards all lending institutions.

The Holdup

A crowded bank. A teller stands behind the counter, counting money. A robber, wearing a mask and carrying a gun, enters. He waves the gun. He jumps up and down. He falls on the floor in a fit and writhes and moans. Finally, he coughs and clears his throat. The teller glances up.

Teller

May I help you, sir?

Robber

Yes, please. This is a holdup. Give me all your money.

Teller

Yes, I see. Could you please try the next window? I'm embezzling.

Robber

Oh, right.

The robber moves to the next window where teller #2 stands waiting.

Teller #2

May I help you, sir?

The robber hands him a note.

Teller #2

Reading the note.

Please do not panic.

He hands the note back to the robber.

Teller #2

Pleasantly.

Thank you sir, I won't panic.

The robber pushes the note back to the teller.

Robber

Go on, then, read it. There's more.

Teller #2

Looking at note.

That's all it says, sir: "Do not panic."

Robber

Must be on the reverse.

101

Teller #2

Flips card over, reads.

Coffee, sugar, mayonnaise...

Robber

Below that.

Teller #2

Oh. "I have a gun."

Teller looks up at the robber with a blank expression.

Robber

...and...

Teller #2

"And" what, sir?

Robber

Read the rest of the note.

Teller #2

That's all there is, sir. "Do not panic, I have a gun."

Robber

What?! Let me see that.

He snatches the note and scans it quickly.

Robber

Exasperated.

Honestly, I can't trust that bloody wife of mine to do one simple thing! All I say to her is "Dear, please be sure to write the holdup note," but she can't tear herself away from her bloody soap operas long enough to help me earn a bloody living! How I'm supposed to get ahead I'll never know. Tch...women!

Teller #2

I know what you mean, sir.

Robber

Yes, well, enough of this gay banter. Please hand over all of your money now or I'll have to shoot you.

Teller #2

I see. May I see the gun in question, sir?

The robber sticks the gun under the teller's nose.

Teller #2

Is this the gun mentioned in the note, sir?

Robber

Well of *course* it is, you twit. What other gun would it *be?* Now please hand over all your money or I'll really have to shoot you.

CRAHAM crackers

Teller #2

Of course, sir. May I inquire as to whether or not you have an account with us?

Robber

No, I don't have a bloody account with you, you boob! Give me the money or I'll blow your silly head off!

Teller #2

Well that's going to be a little difficult as you don't have an account with us. I'm afraid it's bank policy.

Looking past the robber.

Next!

Robber

It's bank policy for you to get your *head* blown off?

Teller #2

I'm sorry sir, but it's the rule. Would you care to open an account?

Robber

Disgusted.

Oh, shut up and leave me alone.

Teller #2

Oh, you'd like a *loan!* Do you have any collateral?

Robber

Incredulously.

I have a *gun!*

Teller #2

Yes, and it's a very *nice* gun, indeed, sir, but I don't think it will be *quite* enough security.

Robber

Completely fed up.

Look, I don't want a loan, and I don't want to open an account. What I want is for you to open your drawer and give me all of the money inside it!

Teller #2

Stupefied.

What, *give* it to you? For *free?*

Robber

Yes, that's right.

Teller #2

Why, I've never *heard* of such a thing. Do you realize what would happen if we just *gave*

money to everyone who marched in here with a
gun and demanded it?

Robber

Yes, the bank would finally be providing a
worthwhile service...

Teller #2

No, sir, it would be anarchy! There'd be no
forms to fill out, nothing to process and file—I'd
be out of a job! Look, I'm sorry, but I can't give
you *any* money unless you've—one—already *got*
an account with us or—two—fill out the proper
forms and make a proper deposit. It's more
than my job's worth, sir.

Robber

I give up. How much to open an account?

Teller #2

Fifty dollars.

Robber

Handing him some bills.

Here you go.

Teller #2

Thank you, sir. Is there anything else I can do
for you today?

Pythonesque sketches you've never seen...

The robber levels his gun at the teller's nose.

Robber
Give me fifty dollars or I'll blow your brains out.

CHAPTER 12

What's the point of writing an autobiography if you don't die?

At the age of 36, I thought I would start writing my autobiography. Because of my dependence on alcohol, I honestly didn't think that I was going to last much longer. It didn't *disturb* me that I was going to perhaps be dead in three or four years. In fact, I thought I'd die at the age of 42.[1] At least, that's

---

[1] Douglas Adams fans take note: The answer to the question, "What is the meaning of life, the universe, and everything?", as revealed in *A Hitchhiker's Guide to the Galaxy*, is also 42. Coincidence? No. Graham, a longtime friend, said "42" when Adams asked him for the answer to the above question. Adams has since denied this.

---

what I thought then, and it didn't worry me at all. Stupid, isn't it? But there we are.

So I started to write this little autobiography just to get a few things down, really, but I found that the writing wasn't progressing very quickly. This was because I was drinking quite torrentially at that point. But after I'd sobered up, the writing progressed much quicker and I actually found it was an enjoyable and cathartic experience to have to think back upon my life, how this had all happened in the first place, and to write it down.

The reason I called the book A Liar's Autobiography was because I realized very early on that it's almost impossible to tell the truth. Not impossible because of any reasons of libel (although a title like A Liar's Autobiography certainly would help protect me in some measure), but because *truth changes*. I know that sounds like nonsense but the truth is that truth—that which is true to you—three or four years later, when you look back at the same situation from a different perspective, could be very different indeed.

I began to realize this fact while writing the book. So, since I couldn't really swear that I was right, particularly with all that alcohol that had gone inside me, I decided the truthful thing would be to call it A Liar's Autobiography. Also, since I was contemplating writing it with other people, I thought that that title would be a good way to get me out of the problem of writing an autobiography with several co-authors.[2]

---

[2] Co-authors include Douglas Adams, Alex Martin, David Yallop, and Graham's longtime companion, writer David Sherlock.

In the end, of course, it turned out that I *didn't* die at the age of 42, and so the entire point of the autobiography was somewhat lost. Instead I fortunately knocked booze on the head and have since spent the past 11 years as sober as a judge, thank you very much. While I am obviously delighted by the fact that I *didn't* die at age 42, it *did* leave me somewhat embarrassed as I'd made such an issue out it. Oh, well, you can't lose them all.

An excerpt from

A Liar's Autobiography

Screenplay by David Sherlock and Jim Yoakum
Based upon the book by Graham Chapman, David Sherlock,
Alex Martin, David Yallop and Douglas Adams
©1994, 1997 White Bike Productions, Ltd. Registered WGA

Exterior. Streets of Hampstead—evening.

The moon is beaming, the streets are empty, the odors of rose bay, willow herb, night-scented stock and dog shit vie with each other for dominance. David Sherlock is moving down the street, walking off his anger.

A moment later, he is joined by Graham, who has sprinted the last few steps in order to catch him. They walk together in silence until their way is blocked by a large peony bush that hangs over someone's garden fence. Graham reaches up and brushes it away, somewhat brusquely.

David

Irritated.

Don't be so rough! They're pretty.

Graham

What are?

David

The peonies.

David reaches up and plucks one.

David

See?

The still night air is shattered by the sound of a wailing police siren. We hear a screech of brakes and behind Graham and David we see a police car slam to a halt and two policemen get out. One of them, a brute of a man wearing small, owlish glasses, snatches the flower from David's hands. His name is Piggy.

Piggy

Right! What's all this then?

Graham

It's a peony.

Piggy

Oh, so you *admit* that then?

He looks knowingly over at the other policeman, a man named Carver, who writes this down in his notebook.

Graham

Admit it? But look, officer...

Piggy

Oh, don't you try and flatter *me*! You won't get out of it *that* way, my lad.

David

Get out of what?

Carver

Deadly tone.

Calm down.

Graham

Look, please, what am I supposed to have done?

Piggy

Not you—(motions with his head to David)— him. He's committed a felony.

Graham is starting to get irritated.

Graham

What?! What do you mean "a felony"?

Piggy

Theft, that's what I mean. He has taken away the personal goods of another, viz., one peony.

He holds up the flower and shows it 'round.

Graham

But it's only a flower...

Carver

Flabbergasted.

Only a flower?! Ho! Ho! That, my lad, is *property*!

Piggy

Nodding.

Property.

Graham

What do you mean, "property"?

Piggy

Did this peony just appear out of thin air, sir?

David

No, it came from that bush.

Piggy

Pointing.

That bush there?

To David.

Is that bush yours?

David

No, of course it isn't...

Piggy

To Graham.

Is that bush yours?

Graham

No. Now look, this is all rather...

Carver

Is that bush the bush of a friend or relation?

Graham

Sighing.

No...

Piggy

Aha! Then it is "another's"! Did you ask the permission of "another" before you picked his or her peony?

Graham

No...

Piggy and Carver exchange looks—they've got them!

Piggy

Then that, my lad, is theft, which is a felony and punishable with up to 30 years imprisonment in Her Majesty's prison at Wormwood Scrubs!

116

As Piggy and Carver write down the charges with glee, we see an old lady being beaten up by four thugs; innocent passersby being attacked and robbed at random; men wearing ski masks running out of houses with big bags marked "LOOT" behind them. The fuzz are oblivious.

Graham

Look, my friend just picked a bloody flower!!!

Piggy

Stole a flower.

Graham

All right, fine then, *stole* a flower. We'll just put it back then.

Carver

"Put it back," sir? And how would you intend to do that? It's been *severed*.

Graham realizes the quandary.

Piggy

Perhaps he's going to sellotape it back, eh?

Carver

Yeah. Or maybe with a few well-placed rivets.

He and Piggy chuckle.

Graham

Okay, fine, since we obviously can't put it back, then we'll buy them a whole new bush.

Piggy

You can't do that.

David

Why not?

Piggy

Obvious. It wouldn't be the *same* bush, now would it?

Graham

Well, no. But if you're going to get technical about it, I think you should note that this bush was obstructing the pavement!

Piggy closes his notebook and narrows his eyes. He moves in closer to Graham.

Piggy

Here, you wouldn't be trying to be *clever*, would you?

Graham

Well no, it's just that...Look, it's only a bloody flower!

Carver

I think we may have to take him down to the station and be "interviewed."

To Graham.

It can be very nasty, being "interviewed."

Graham backs away.

Graham

Are you threatening violence?

Piggy

Right, send for reinforcements!

Carver

On radio.

Attention all cars! Attention all cars! There's been a peony-severance in Hampstead! We need reinforcements...

We hear the sound of approaching sirens.

PART THREE

Outright Lies

(Well, not really blatant. And perhaps lies is a bit
strong. But then we have to be consistent, don't we, bit of
editorial integrity and all that, so calling it Random
Dissemblings or Vague Memories That Just Might Be
Almost True wouldn't work now, would it?)

CHAPTER 13

How to build a birdhouse

Book One: Start with wood and a naked Chinese lady

According to Jim Yoakum, "How to Build a Birdhouse" simply appeared one day via the fax machine. Many months earlier, Jim reports, he and Graham had discussed his college lecture tours. He recounts, "I had made the suggestion that they would make a fascinating concert film. (I had recently seen Spalding Gray's "Swimming to Cambodia" and pointed to its unique style and lighting techniques as an example of how it could be done.) He was unconvinced. At the very least, I said, they should be incorporated somehow into a book (not unlike this one), especially as his manuscript for A Liar's Autobiography Part II *had just been stolen. I suggested a silly how-to book, and mentioned* How to Build a Canoe *as a possibility. He didn't comment one way or the other. Later, I received this...in five parts."*

Preparing the stock

Building a birdhouse is not only fun and educational, it's a great way to use up all those smaller, extraneous bits of wood scraps that end up gathering dust in the far corner of the hobby shop because we don't know what to do with them. Well, now you do. Or you will. Or won't. Whatever.

Before we begin sawing, make sure that your work area is free of clutter. After all, as Oscar "Ozzie" Wilde never once said, "A cluttered hobby shop is the Devil's hobby shop." So if you've been looking for a good excuse to toss out all those rusty old anvils and scimitars and back issues of *Illustrated Goat Herder's Monthly*—this is it. This is also a good time to take a moment to put out any small, unattended fires that are blazing away in the corner, as they will only prove to be a nuisance while you try to work.

Okay, now that you've gotten your work area "ship shape" (or "hobby-shop shape," more like), it's time to talk about wood! Oak, pine, larch—any good tree-grown wood will do for this project. I suggest that if you plane or resaw 3/4"-thick stock down, then be certain to start with pieces at least 18" long for safe planing or sawing and bring them down to 1/4" or 3/8" thickness.

The thickness isn't critical. However, safety *is*, so take an-other quick look around your work area. Is it safe? Absolutely rat-free? Fires out? Are you *sure*? Good.

We're going to make the outside dimensions of the bird box parts in increments. I favour the larger sort of birdhouse, with a box that's about 16" square. Give them plenty of room to flap about, I say! So that's what we're going to build. Ready?

Here's a checklist of items we'll need for our birdhouse:

1. Wood (very important!)
2. Saws, clamps, work tables, and other tools or tool-related items
3. A naked Chinese lady

To begin, dim the lights and take off all of your clothing. Now lay back on the couch (making certain to cover your naughty bits with a piece of cloth), close your eyes, and relax. I personally find that trying to mentally name all the great Scottish bowlers helps me nod off. Next, instruct the naked Chinese lady to take a small dab of highly scented kama-sutra oil and massage it gently into your chest and shoulder area, using erotic, swirling, counter-clockwise motions. Now, gently switch on the vibrator (making certain not to disturb the yak) and insert it into your...[1]

First rip your stock to these widths on your table saw—*but not before making certain that there are no violent tornadoes approaching from the far corner of your work area!* Everything okay? Good. Whew. You can never be too careful.

Put your blade at a 90-degree angle and *carefully* rip along the long grain on the edges of your stock. Did you do that? You

---

[1] This particular paragraph has absolutely NOTHING to do with building a birdhouse and by following it you may very well end up in either: a) jail or b) traction. It is actually from the foreword of the book, *How to Build an Erection* by Cpt. Hugh Jampton and was included here by accident. (Copies of *How to Build an Erection* can be obtained from the author for £5.60 or three years in prison, whichever is cheaper.)

didn't inadvertently saw off an arm or anything, did you? Because it will only serve to slow the project down if you did. Both arms intact? How's the Chinese lady?[2] Good.

Now, set up your table cutoff box with the blade tilted to a 45-degree angle so you can cut the miters on the parts. It is very important that you use a toggle clamp to hold the parts as you do this, otherwise the parts may fly off in all directions and cause a panic in the streets! This happened once in Hampstead, back in 1964, and the Army had to be brought out to restore order![3]

Speaking of dangerous things, this might be a good time to tell you about my adventures with an *ad hoc* group called the Dangerous Sports Club. Actually, it might be a totally inappropriate time to do so, but since it's my book, I really don't care if you don't agree, so I'm going to do it anyway.

---

2 This sentence should be removed so as not to confuse the reader. See previous footnote.

3 Read *Restoring Order in Hampstead (And Other Exciting Local Events Viewed From the Window of My Sweets Shop)* by Betty Maynard (Mrs.).

CHAPTER 14

The Dangerous Sports Club: A Python on skis

A couple of years ago, I was sitting at home, trying to write, when I had a telephone call from a British newspaper called *The Daily Mail*. Now *The Mail* is not one of our *better* newspapers (not the worst, either, sad to say) but they irritated me in that they wanted to know what I would do if I won their £1 million bingo competition. I immediately replied that I would give it to John Cleese so that he could take the afternoon off. They thought that was quite funny, but a little cruel, and printed a watered-down version of the joke in the newspaper the next day, which annoyed me intensely. But they also mentioned that I would like to go to the Andes.

Now I had, in fact, mentioned the Andes in talking to them, because I used to climb a little bit. Well, the same day that this article appeared, I had a telephone call from a gentleman called David Kirke who said he was the chairman of the Dangerous Sports Club, and he wondered if I would like to go hang gliding over active volcanoes in Ecuador. I said, "Ummmmmmmmmnnnnnnnnno..."

Ummmmmmyesssssss!

But I *was* kind of interested in that I hadn't had many phone calls like that before and so I chatted with the man a little bit. All I knew about the Dangerous Sports Club at that point had been gleaned from seeing excerpts of some of their activities on television. Anyway, I chatted with the man a bit, and got to know a little more about the group, and subsequently *did* agree to go to Ecuador with them.

I realized at the time that I was probably being invited along as some sort of a useless mascot, perhaps to gain a little extra sponsorship money, that sort of thing, and so I agreed that I'd go for only one week (I said that I'd arranged lots of important meetings. It was all totally fictitious, of course, but I wanted to make sure that my time there was going to be limited, so that the chances of my having to do anything *actually dangerous* were also limited.)

Now Ecuador is quite a tall sort of place. Quito, the capital city, is some 10,000 feet above sea level, and once there I found that simply bending down to tie up my shoelaces gave me quite a headache. I imagined that climbing any of the mountains around there in order to hang glide off of them would involve a little bit in the way of acclimatization to altitude, because a lot of volcanoes in that country are 20,000 feet or so in height. But, of course, the Dangerous Sports Club doesn't believe in acclimatization. They would prefer to do things with the headaches.

Towards the end of that week I thought I was going to get away with not having done anything at all dangerous, but then they suggested that perhaps I should climb up one mountain with them, a mountain called Cotopaxi, which is somewhat over 20,000 feet in height.

We have to climb it *when?*

Cotopaxi is a volcano, meaning it has that sort of shape, and therefore it's not technically difficult as a climb. However it *is* rather tall. Height aside, the main problem about climbing this mountain is that you have to climb it *at night*. This is because it's on the equator, and if you're on the mountain after about, ooh... eight o'clock in the morning...then the sun begins to melt the snow and ice above you, and the melted sludge then tends to fall on you.

So, at about eleven o'clock at night, four of us set out from our mountaineering post located at about 15,000 feet and (with considerable headaches) began to climb on up. I must say that it was one of the most physically exhausting things I've ever attempted. It really was a matter of taking six *incredibly* deep breaths every step because none of us were acclimatized, and we all had wonderful thumping headaches.

We got to within about 1,000 feet of the summit when, suddenly, one of the group developed altitude sickness, and the only sensible thing to do was come back down again. It was just as well since the leader of the group had lost his way anyhow. It didn't really matter that we never reached the summit as the real reason for this little jaunt had been to discover just how difficult it was going to be to carry hang gliders to the top.

Obviously, the answer was "very."

Guilt is a curious thing

Shortly afterwards I left and returned to England. The group stayed on, though, and subsequently managed to make it to the top of Mt. Chimborazo, which is even higher than Cotopaxi. They even managed to carry some hang gliders to the summit, though once they reached it they found that the snow was well above waist deep and they couldn't run to take off. So they hung around up there long enough to get frostbite, and then they came back down again.

Although that expedition was not particularly successful from a hang-gliding point of view, the Dangerous Sports Club does intend to go back, as there's one mountain they have their eyes on. It's called Sangay, and it's very much the sort of place that the members of the club are aiming for, as it conveniently erupts every 10 minutes or so—poisonous gases, red-hot boulders rolling down, lava casually sauntering along at 30 miles per hour. I don't know whether or not I shall join them on that expedition.

Anyway, as I said, I left and arrived back in England unscathed, but I quickly began to feel guilty that I'd been made a member of this club and hadn't actually done anything dangerous. A curious sort of guilt, I grant you. But I was pleased that I had gotten to know this group of people, and was surprised to find that they were really a very varied crowd.

On the one hand, there were the usual out-of-work English persons, while on the other, there was, well, a member of the British aristocracy, I suppose, a kind of third cousin to Queen Elizabeth with the extraordinary name of Zan Fitz-Allen Herbert. He really gave meaning to the word "inbred," as he was essentially a loony. A very *nice* loony, I grant you, but a complete whacko nonetheless.

In between those two extremes were quite a variety of people, everything from farmers to stockbrokers, all sorts of people who had only one thing in common—they all liked to do things which scared them a bit. Things to which an unacceptable risk was attached. Things that "normal people" (like you) would consider downright dangerous and stupid.

Anyway, I decided that I would go with them to St. Moritz, Switzerland, for their winter sports festival, knowing full well that I would be adult enough to say "no" if anything they'd planned looked too stupid or too dangerous. I was determined that I wasn't going to succumb to peer pressure and take part in something which would end in injury. Or worse.

So I arrived in Switzerland only to find that the Dangerous Sports Club was already in trouble. In fact, they hadn't even been allowed into the *country* yet. It seems that they'd been prevented access because David Kirke hadn't paid his hospital bill from the previous year. Well, it was all cleared up and, before long, I found myself at the top of a mountain, staring down—a very *long* down, I might add.

Of black ski runs and brown trousers

Now, describing the Dangerous Sports Club's Winter Sport is simple: It is an uncontrolled descent of a snow slope on skis. The intriguing (and dangerous) part is that there has to be *something* interposed between yourself and the skis, thus rendering control utterly impossible. The normal method of stopping being "The Crash." Points are given for imagination in terms of what it is that's placed between yourself and the skis—anything from a wheelchair to a grand piano.

So there I found them, at the top of this mountain, grumbling to the organizers that they'd been given "too gentle a slope." Now it looked fine to me! I had absolutely *no* problems with it. But it apparently wasn't steep enough, or bumpy enough, or interesting enough, for them, and so they *insisted* on another one.

The organizers agreed to give us another slope, which (unfortunately for me) turned out to be the end of a black ski run. Now, for those of you who aren't aware, a black ski run is the absolute nastiest kind of ski run, the most senior sort. Naturally, it turned out to be a *lot* steeper with a *lot* more bumps on it and, as an added "bonus," it had no run-off area at the bottom. There was just a short, sharp drop with some very dangerous-looking, spiky trees poking up.

I was getting ready to be *very* adult about this.

The item that the club had chosen for me to go down the slope on was an operating table—on skis. I suppose they thought it was appropriate because of my medical background. Now I don't know how much you know about operating tables, but they are rather heavy, metallic objects, and this one was no exception.

I must confess that the idea of lying flat on my back on this thing, staring up at the sky while hurtling down a black ski run at 500 miles per hour did *not* appeal. So I was very adult about it and said, "No, I won't go down on that thing, thank you very much."

But that made me feel guilty again, so I looked around for something else to go down the mountain on. I was searching for the *slowest-looking* vehicle, which turned out to be a 15-foot-long wooden Venetian gondola (which the club had evidently "borrowed" from some local Italian restaurant). In my mind, I felt that the gondola was not only big, cumbersome, and slow, but (most importantly) there were no nasty metal bits sticking out of it.

So we began. The first 10 or so members of the Dangerous Sports Club set off down the slope on various items, all at frightening speed. As it transpired, only one of the 10 was lucky enough to actually reach the bottom, and he was *very* fortunate in that he managed to hit a tree and be thrown several yards into the air.

The next item down the slope was a full-scale replica of a cruise missile, which had two people on board. Because of the missile's detailed design, it proved to be very aerodynamic and successfully reached the bottom of the slope in a matter of seconds. They, too, were very fortunate in that they managed to stop when the front of their machine crumpled upon impact with a large boulder.

So far, so good. No real injuries yet, just a few large purple bruises, minor scratches, and so on. However, the next person down the slope would not prove to be quite so fortunate. The man in question had chosen as his vehicle a Formula 3 race car. While it didn't have its skin—its outer shell—it was *still basically a Formula 3 race car* and (of course) these machines are designed to withstand impact while reaching speeds of Mach 7. Because he felt so safe, he didn't want to wear his safety harness. He thought it would be much better for him if he was actually thrown out of the vehicle. He also wasn't too keen to wear his safety helmet, but all of us eventually persuaded him to wear it.

Anyway, he set off down the slope and began to gather up considerable speed. About two-thirds of the way down, the vehicle caught on some projection or other, and he promptly turned three or four horrendous cartwheels and was, indeed, thrown out of the car. Unfortunately, part of the steering wheel passed through his left thigh as he was leaving the vehicle and the mangled mess (him) eventually came to rest, in a heap, on the ground. He didn't move for several minutes.

About four minutes later the paramedics on skis arrived at the scene, just as he was beginning to stagger to his feet. As it transpired, while he (miraculously) suffered no lasting injuries, he *did* suffer a loss of memory for some five days afterward, something (I was told) that happened to him every year. It then occurred to me that that was probably why he continued to turn up every season—he'd completely forgotten what happened to him all the other times!

Anyway this little crash had cast quite a pall over the proceedings, particularly among the spectators, and so David Kirke decided that, as chairman of the club, he ought to go down the slope next just to cheer everyone up. David's chosen vehicle was a C-5, which is a little electric car developed by an Englishman called Clyde Sinclair. The car had not proved to be a very commercial success, as it was very slow, but on skis the C-5 was *very* aerodynamic.

David whizzed down the slope at 1,500 miles per hour, immediately hit some projection, came to an abrupt halt, and didn't move for several minutes. When he eventually managed to get out of the vehicle, he staggered around for a bit and dabbed at the trickle of blood spurting from his left temple.

Oh, solo mio!

It was my turn next.

Now normally I would have considered this a good time to run to the nearest bar or inn or convent—any place whose inhabitants considered it mad to risk life and limb on a ski slope. Well, I discovered, "peer pressure" is a truly nasty beast, for the next thing I knew, I was sitting optimistically in the back of the gondola. No, optimistic is the wrong word, really. *Worried* is more like it. I looked around and noticed that sitting next to me was Zan Fitz-Allen Herbert. Not much comfort there. Zan turned to me and, smiling, said, "Looks like a bit of a brown trouser job this afternoon." Which did little to improve my state of mind.

Also sitting with us, in the front of the gondola, was Eric. Now Eric is the Dangerous Sports Club's mascot, and he is in the shape of a man totally bandaged from head to foot. He is always smoking a little cigarette and (for some reason or other) wears a pair of boxer shorts, beneath which is what can only be described as *an erection*. A rather *mobile* erection. They use Eric to annoy people in restaurants. A job at which he is singularly successful.

So there we were—Zan, myself, and Eric. We were pushed off from the top of this slope, in this gondola, and (much to my consternation) we began to gather considerable speed. By the second bump, we were airborne! The thought "broken leg" immediately flashed through my mind. I soon found myself flying over Zan's head. Then I noticed Zan flying over *my* head, followed by Eric, who was making a beeline straight at me, his little wooden mobile erection heading straight for my ~!

Soon we were all sliding down the slippery slope, being pursued by this wretched wooden gondola, desperately kicking at it to avoid further injury. Eventually we managed to reach the bottom of the slope where Zan, myself, and Eric finished up badly winded—but alive! (Except for Eric, of course.) And that felt great. I mean, I was thoroughly elated, totally full of adrenaline. The incident really put the whole world into perspective for me. I felt good for about two weeks after the event.

I was glad that one downhill event *didn't* take place that afternoon, one that involved a London double-decker bus Zan had brought along on which he had fitted enormous, specially commissioned skis. He suggested it would be a great idea if, at the end of the afternoon, we all piled into this bus and...

I thought not.

In fact the local mayor thought not as well, as there was an election that week and he was worried about giving his opponent the "ecology issue," in that damage might be caused to certain trees—and fences, houses, and hotels.

CHAPTER 15

How to build a birdhouse

Book Two: Getting the groove in your bottom

Cutting the grooves

Now I hope that you were able to move the toggle clamp without too much injury (see Book One). If not, remember that a pressure bandage is the best way to stop any bleeding.[1] Simply place a gauze pad directly over the wound, then apply the bandage over it. Any clean strip of material can be used for a bandage—Evan Picone sheets, Gloria Vanderbilt pillow cases, even

---

[1] Remembering, of course, that the absolute *best* way to stop any bleeding is to not get injured in the first place.

those silly little ruffle-things-that-go-between-the-box-springs-and-the-mattress-that-don't-seem-to-actually-do-anything-except-gather-dust can be used.

If, for some reason, you seem to have severely gashed yourself in a room where expensive designer bed linen is not kept, then by all means use whatever is handy—cheaper poly-cotton blend sheets can do in a pinch, old woolen socks with half the heel missing, even the pages of many inexpensive magazines can be torn into strips and used as bandages in an emergency situation. (Come to think of it, maybe you *shouldn't* have tossed out all those back issues of *Illustrated Goat Herder's Monthly*, after all.)

Once the bleeding has stopped, and after you've filled out all of the proper medical forms, we can move on to the next step, which is cutting grooves on the box sides for our bottom.[2] I suggest that you use 1/8" plywood for the box bottom. Or use 1/4" plywood if that's all you have. You can even use stiff card-board if you want. I really don't care. It's really not that impor-tant, and the birds won't know the difference.

Now, use your table saw or your router to cut a groove on the bottom inside edge of the box side. Locate the groove about 3/16" above the bottom edge and make certain its width matches the thickness of your bottom.[3] You can use a push stick to help guide the parts across the cutter. Now, glue the four sides of the box together, ensuring that all the corners line

---

2 By this, of course, I mean the bottom of the *bird box* and not our *derrieres*. A lesson learnt painfully, you can be assured.

3 You *know* what I mean...

up well and that the box is close to square before setting it aside to dry.

While we're waiting for your box to dry out, let me tell you more about my adventures with the Dangerous Sports Club.

CHAPTER 16

The Dangerous Sports Club: In the nature of a catapulting event

So, anyway, after the Winter Sports adventure I arrived back in England. While I certainly now knew "the buzz" you could get from these activities, I was still by no means hooked. Yet. In fact, it was another year before I agreed to take part in another one of their activities, which happened to be in the nature of a catapulting event.

Now this was for charity and was held in Hyde Park, in London, as part of Bob Geldof's "Sport Aid Day for Africa." I didn't really want to hang around and have to put up with a lot of "brown trouser" talk, so I arrived late in the hope that they would be absolutely ready for me—and indeed they were.

I arrived in Hyde Park and was immediately put into this climbing harness. Then an enormous 150-foot crane lowered down three strands of aircraft carrier elastic, the sort of heavy-duty stuff they use to stop fighter planes from falling off the end of aircraft carriers. That was attached to the front of my flying harness, and then, from behind, I was attached by another rope to a large concrete block set in the ground. The crane was then raised up to its full height.

Avoiding whiplash, strangulation and loss of an eye

The man standing next to me said, "There are one or two things you ought to know. You will be experiencing a force of 6 Gs, so you'll have to hold your hands behind your head like this, otherwise you *will* get whiplash." Not *might*, but *will*, I noted.

"When you get to the top of your flight, you'll notice these coils of rope sort of "floating around" beside you. Don't get tangled up in those or you'll strangle yourself. And then, when you get to the bottom of your flight, remember to hold your arm in front of your face, otherwise the rope could smash you in the nose. One of our guys lost partial sight in one eye the other week."

While I was just beginning to absorb the enormity of these so-called instructions, he said, "Count to five."

I don't remember getting any further than "four" when the decision was taken out of my hands, the rope behind me was slashed with a knife, and I just went

ZIIIIIINNNNNGGGG!!!

And I don't remember much about the way up, either.

It was all so very quick. But I *do* remember arriving at the top of my arc and floating around for what seemed like an age! And, sure enough, I saw these coils of rope floating around beside me, and I thought, "Well *surely* by now I should be..."

And then I was.

Being so full of adrenaline I certainly did remember to hold my arm in front of my face, preventing any possible damage that way, and then I found myself merely bouncing up and down on the end of the rope, and I was able to do kind of moon hops on the ground. Again, I felt thoroughly exhilarated! It was like the best fairground ride I'd ever had!

They'd been quite kind to me, since, in their eyes, 6 Gs wasn't too bad. And I'd only gone up to a height of about 130 feet or so. They quite regularly "enjoy" activities that exert far more than 6 Gs of force, even going up to 11 Gs, which is practically black-out time. But they were kind to me. Thankfully. However I haven't yet taken part in my third activity, which I suppose I will have to do at some point—bungee jumping from a bridge.

If the ground looks like concrete, run away!

I did go along with them again one afternoon, to a village in Oxfordshire, with the thought that I might take part in a little local charity event. David Kirke again had a huge crane there. He was going to do bungee jumping from a bucket suspended from this 150-foot crane. I went up in the bucket with him, to see what the ground looked like from up above, and to me it looked like concrete.

I began to have some doubts at that point. So I descended and David went back up again with a sack full of bricks weighing about the same as himself, just to test out the rope. He tied the sack to the rope and threw it out from the bucket where it promptly smashed to pieces on the concrete. I thought, "Perhaps this isn't the afternoon for me to do this particular event."

So a third event is still sometime in the future for me. Although I've insisted that it be over water.

I've also decided that the Dangerous Sports Club would make a very good subject for an adventure movie, and I have, in fact, written a movie script about them. I think it will be the first adventure movie without special effects.

Or insurance.

CHAPTER 17

How to build a birdhouse

Book Three:
Filling out the forms

Cutting key joints

Our box should be dry, so it's time to cut our key joints. I suggest cutting the dovetail key joints in the box corners with a procedure that involves cutting slots for splines in the miter joints at the table saw, but you can also use a simple dovetail bit in your router, if you'd like.

Cut a 45-degree angle into a piece of lumber at least 1 3/4" thick and 18" long at your table saw. I don't know why you do this, it's just the way I learned it, so I'm passing it on to you. If you want, you can throw the lumber away once you've made the cut, or you can put it aside to build other birdhouses. I don't care. And, frankly, neither should you.

Raise the bit to a height equal to the width of the miter joints, multiplied by the average yearly rainfall in Barming, minus 10. I don't know why, but the answer always invariably comes out to 3.1416, so you can either do the math or apply Parkinson's Shortcut® and simply raise the bit 1/16". It's up to you.

Now comes the difficult bit. Use the toggle clamp to hold the birdhouse in place and give it dovetail keys, while simultaneously drafting a letter to the local building council asking for the required permits needed to erect your birdhouse. As this permission will invariably take days, weeks, even months to not arrive, it is imperative that you write now for the proper forms and licenses to fill out so that they can be ignored as soon as possible. I know of a fellow who waited until he'd already finished his birdhouse before writing to the council, and his not-grantal-of-permission took twice as long to not arrive as someone's who'd written to the council at birth.

While we wait for the proper forms to be filled out, filed away, and properly ignored, and since I have absolutely nothing further to say about dangerous sports of any kind, allow me say a few words about the most dangerous *man* I ever knew. (Which my editor has assured me is a really keen, tricky way to get readers to turn the page and actually believe there is a method behind the madness of this book. Kind of a Dickensian twist, if you will. That should be "Dikkens," with two "Ks," the well-known Dutch author.)

CHAPTER 18

The world's most dangerous man: The Who's Keith Moon (Dux)

I seem to make a habit of getting involved with dangerous people in one way or another, so I guess it's not surprising that one of my dear friends, unfortunately no longer with us, was a gentleman by the name of Keith Moon, who was, of course, the drummer for The Who. Quite a wild character, indeed.

I first met Keith at a charity soccer match in England. It was, in fact, billed as "Monty Python Versus the Rest of the World," and Keith was playing for the "Rest of the World."

I didn't play soccer, I used to play rugby football, so I was rather bored with the intense interest the other people seemed to be taking in this soccer game. It was all rather serious. *I thought that, on the whole, the audience had come out there to see us all make fools of ourselves!* With that in mind, I'd gone along dressed as the Colonel[1] and proceeded to generally make a nuisance of myself—walking around, barking orders, shouting at people, standing in the goal mouth and being as obstructive as possible.[2]

Keith must have felt similarly bored because he left the field at one point and then drove back on in someone's car—and proceeded to score *several* goals! No one could catch him. That led to a kind of instant rapport between the two of us, so we went to a bar and drank *very very very very very very very* many drinks together.[3]

Would *you* rent a hotel room to this man?

The next time I met Keith, he was staying at a London hotel called the Londonderry. While it is not a particularly huge or eminently respectable hotel, it was, in fact, the *only hotel in London which would allow Keith to stay*, as he had a

---

[1] "The Colonel" has absolutely nothing to do with either Colonel Tom Parker or Colonel Sanders (to answer the two silliest questions for the 845th time). He was an RAF-type character who used to swagger into skits on the "Monty Python" TV shows and shout, "Too silly!" when things were (indeed) getting rather silly.

[2] On the whole, not a bad way to play soccer.

[3] Read *The World's Greatest Bar Tabs Volume VI* (Sot Press) by E.W. Shepherd-Walwyn for complete details.

---

rather peculiar habit of destroying hotel rooms.[4] He had registered under the name of "Rupert Wilde" and taken one of the penthouses.

I arrived on the top floor and knocked on Keith's door. Keith opened it, so I entered. I immediately noticed that there were two or three Swedish girls in the room. I don't know what they were doing in there—probably helping him tidy up or something.

Keith immediately apologized to me, saying that he had no gin in the room—gin being my lubricant of choice at the time—and handing me a bottle of lager to "get on with" while he rang down to room service and asked them to send up a bottle of gin. Well, some 10 minutes—and about four or five lagers—later, he noticed that there was *still* no sign of this gin arriving in the room, so he rang room service again and told them that "if the gin doesn't appear in my room within the next five minutes, then your television set will appear on the pavement." Keith was *very* strict like that.

A few minutes passed, I was halfway through another lager, and there was still no sign of the gin. So Keith wandered over to the side of the room and promptly climbed out of the window onto (what I assumed) was a balcony outside. I didn't know what he was up to, but I was halfway through a lager so I wasn't too bothered—I mean, Keith did things like that pretty

---

4 Keith (and The Who) were banned for life from the Holiday Inn chain for various offenses committed while residing there on tour. Among the many things Keith did while staying there over the years was drive a limousine into a swimming pool, throw various television sets out of the windows, construct and cement a large brick dog kennel to the floor, and nail all the furniture to the ceiling.

much as a matter of course. A few minutes later, there was still no sign of him coming back in, so I wandered over to the window to have a look-see at what he was doing out there.

The first thing I noticed was that there *wasn't* a balcony, just a ledge about four or five inches wide, no more, and about four feet beneath the window. Of course, there was also no sign of Keith, though there was (thankfully) no mess on the pavement beneath.

Evidently, Keith was climbing around the building on this ledge! It was certainly something *I* would never have contemplated, but it *was* Keith, so I wasn't too bothered. I sat back down, opened another lager and waited.

After I finished that lager, Keith suddenly reappeared at the window, carrying in his hand a bottle of Beefeater gin. He walked in, plonked it down on the table in front of me, and said, "Here you go, Graham."

He'd made his way along the ledge and promptly burgled the drinks cabinet of the next-door penthouse!

"Well," I thought, "now, *there's* a friend!"

CHAPTER 19

How to build a birdhouse

Book Four: Gouging out the hole

(I must explain that it's usually at about this point in the birdhouse-building process where I get all frustrated at having wasted the better part of an afternoon building a bloody birdhouse. Rest assured that I'm seeing someone about this undefined anger, and we feel that I'm making progress.)

Making a hole in the bloody thing

Now comes the most important part in the building of our birdhouse (taken from the perspective of its future inhabitants, that is)—the ceremonial drilling of the bird hole.

Now, I *could* natter on and on about which correct bit to use and include all sorts of intricate directions on toggle joints and saws, but really, the easiest way to make a hole is to just take a chisel and gouge one out! Preferably it should be about 3/4" in diameter, so that the birds can enter, although it really doesn't matter. I mean, they're just dirty, stinking birds, so just hack away at the bloody thing until you get a hole the size and feel that *you* like!

While you fiddle about with the hacksaw, I will tell you another interesting tale I just remembered about dear old Keith.

CHAPTER 20

Keith Moon
Redux

Keith often had incidents where he "involved himself" at hotels. My favorite incident occurred while he was staying at a hotel in Los Angeles called the Hyatt House on Sunset Strip.

Keith was returning to the hotel one afternoon, after having rehearsed with the band in the morning, and was listening to a cassette recording of the rehearsal as he walked through the lobby. Evidently he was playing it too loudly and there was some kind of complaint, so the manager approached him and told him to, *ahem*, quote, "turn that noise off."

Well, Keith was a considerate sort, so he immediately obliged the manager, turned off the cassette player and went off to his room...where he happened to have a large supply of detonator caps that he'd been saving for the show later on in the week. He spent the next 20 minutes or so meticulously wiring these caps to the back of his door, then rang the manager and told him he wanted to see him immediately.

Then he waited.

When the manager knocked on the door, Keith did a quick countdown, pushed a lever and blew the whole door off its hinges.

As the amazed manager stared at the smoking doorway, Keith stepped through the rubble, holding his cassette recorder, and said, "*That* (pointing to the bits of door strewn along the hallway) was *noise*, mate. *This* (pointing to the cassette recorder) is 'The fucking Who!'"

I must say, he certainly had a way of dealing with authority figures.

CHAPTER 21

How to build a birdhouse

Book Five: The finished product

Congratulations! It is hoped that you have followed my directions carefully and have received no serious or lasting injuries in the process. If so, then your completed birdhouse should look something like this (Figure 14).

If it doesn't, simply go back to Chapter 13 (Book One) and, instead of setting up your table cutoff box with the blade tilted to a 45-degree angle so you can cut the miters on the parts, set it at *32 degrees* and leave the edges ragged. Add a little pinch of glue and some common binding twine to the miter joints (Photo 3), place the bottom in its groove (Photo 34), and fold the box together (Photo 35). Tape the last joint together (Illustration 55), and then trim it flush with a chisel (Photo 107).

If this *still* doesn't do the trick, by all means, give up.

Falling backward while looking forward

My days as a member of Monty Python represented a period of my life which was both great fun and rather painful. I feel that my problems with alcohol were, in part, related to working with the group, though it's very difficult to say how much was just me and the sheer exuberant joy of excess—being on the edge and overindulging, which is part of my makeup—and how much drinking was an effort to minimize the strain, or to shield me from hurt or to act as Dutch courage. Perhaps it was elements of all these things.

If we were to start all over again, I think I'd enjoy it more. I enjoyed performing and acting in things like *Life of Brian* much more than I did during the television series or the other two movies (*Holy Grail* and *And Now For Something Completely Different*). There was a sort of competitiveness in the group, a certain amount of angling and politicking for roles. I suppose I felt in some respects that, as co-author with John, when it came to casting, perhaps *I* should have had a role in it instead of Michael or John getting it. I'll be honest—it annoyed me. Nobody would ever think of me as having written, say, "The Dead Parrot" sketch, which, in most people's minds, was John and Michael—because they acted in it.

To be fair, at the time I wasn't particularly interested in acting. I thought of myself primarily as a writer. I could create bits of lunacy. Again, cart or horse, I'm not sure, but the result of this was that I tended to spend more time in the bar than was good for me. I didn't want to hang around in rehearsal, trying to make something perfect, which I felt an actor could have come in and done for me. I mean, I could have been enjoying myself in the bar! There was also the occasional hurt that I could have been entrusted with some rather juicy roles, which, of course, I eventually was, so everything came out in the wash, really.

It's not that I felt the others held my drinking against me. In fact I don't think they even noticed it as much as they should have. It's very hard for some people to deal with that kind of problem, but I don't think that they ever saw it as the big problem it probably was. That's because, while I was very open and obvious about my drinking, I was quite good at hiding having a hell of a lot of alcohol inside me and not showing it. I could still function. My tolerance level must have been quite high.

Even so, I don't think to this day that John Cleese quite appreciates what I was actually going through. John was always very punctilious and got very tetchy if somebody was late, and I would constantly be late. I just really wasn't that together—and it didn't worry me at the time, either. Sometimes John would attribute my behavior to irresponsibility, but the truth often was that I'd been rather physically ill. All of it because of drink. Of course, looking back at it, there's no reason for any of them to have known that I was that deeply involved.

As I said, if I were to do Python again, I think that I would enjoy it more because I think (hope) I would have been a little more insistent about roles. They just assumed, "It's okay, Graham won't want it," and many times it was true. I wasn't very good about speaking up—I'm not a very forceful personality—and deep down I didn't think any of that business about roles really mattered. What mattered was the *show*.

It's a curious thing, but I never really felt that Python was what I was here to do. I knew that it was part of my life, but not the whole thing. Even when the television series became a huge hit, I was writing other things that ran concurrently, so Python was never as all-encompassing to me as it was for, say, Michael Palin or Terry Jones. I think this is true for John, too—I don't think Python was quite as much a part of his life as it was for the others.

I feel very fortunate to have weathered all the storms, and I'm looking forward to a bit more smooth sailing. I don't know what I'll do, but I don't think I've done it yet.

I really feel now that I'm about to start my life. Which is very nice.

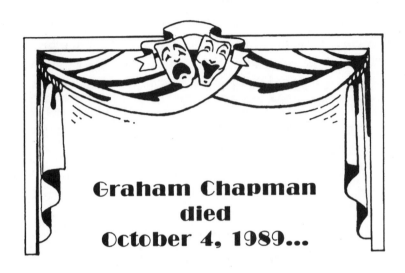

Graham Chapman died October 4, 1989...

One day shy of Python's 20th Anniversary.

Terry Jones called it "the worst case of party-pooping I've ever seen."

Graham Chapman: A life

1941   Born in Leicester on January 8. Father a policeman, mother not.

1953-59 Melton Mowbray Grammar School.

1959-62 Studies Medicine at Emmanuel College, Cambridge. Member of Footlights Club. Footlights Revue (directed by Trevor Nunn).

1962   St. Bartholomew's Hospital, London. Clinical Medicine.

1963   Joins the cast of Footlights Revue in West End. Tour of New Zealand, then three weeks on Broadway, three months off-Broadway.

1966   Writes with John Cleese for "The Frost Report" BBC TV series. Qualified as a doctor. Did not marry. Meets David Sherlock.

         Writes for "The Illustrated Weekly Hudd" BBC TV series and "I'm Sorry I'll Read That Again" BBC Radio.

Writes (with Barry Cryer and Eric Idle) comedy series, "No That's Me Over Here" for Ronnie Corbett.

1967   Writes for "At Last the 1948 Show" and second year of "The Frost Report." Writes for "Marty," Marty Feldman's BBC TV series

1968   Second year "No That's Me Over Here."

Film scripts: *The Magic Christian, The Rise and Rise of Michael Rimmer.*

First TV episode of "Doctor In the House," written with John Cleese, followed by three more with Barry Cryer and five more with Bernard McKenna.

First episodes of "Monty Python's Flying Circus."

1970   Third year "No That's Me Over Here."

Second year "Monty Python's Flying Circus."

Eleven more "Doctor" scripts with Bernard McKenna.

1971   *And Now For Something Completely Different* film.

Monty Python's Big Red Book.

Becomes legal guardian to John Tomiczek.

1972   Third year "Monty Python's Flying Circus."

Writes more Ronnie Corbett shows with Barry Cryer.

Co-founder *Gay News* newspaper.

1973   Python U.K. stage tour. Canadian stage tour.

Brand New Monty Python Book.

1974   Fourth year of "Monty Python's Flying Circus," without John Cleese. Now simply called "Monty Python."

Python stage show, Theatre Royal, Drury Lane, with John Cleese.

Monty Python and the Holy Grail film.

1975   More "Doctor" scripts (with B. McKenna and David Sherlock).

          Fills in between acts for Pink Floyd at Knebworth.

1976   "Monty Python" stage show at the City Center, New York.

          Fills in a bit for The Who at Hammersmith Odeon.

1977   "Out of the Trees" BBC TV.

          "Prince of Denmark" (sitcom) for Ronnie Corbett.

          Stopped drinking alcohol.

1978   Produces, co-scripts, and acts in *The Odd Job* film.

          Monty Python's Life of Brian film.

1979   Co-produces (with Eric Idle) *The Life of Brian* sound-track. *montypythonscrapbook*.

          "The Big Show" NBC TV.

          Appears for a week on "The Hollywood Squares" NBC TV.

1980   *A Liar's Autobiography* is published in hardback.

          Monty Python stage show at the Hollywood Bowl.

          "Monty Python's Contractual Obligation Album."

1981   *A Liar's Autobiography* is published in paperback.

          March 2: First "comedy lecture" at Facets Multimedia, Chicago. Begins lecture tour of 23 U.S. college campuses.

1982   Guest appearance on "Saturday Night Live."

          Monty Python's the Meaning of Life film.

          Screenplay for *Yellowbeard*, an adventure comedy film. Filming is completed in October in Mexico for Orion.

1983   *Monty Python's The Meaning of Life* film, book, and soundtrack released.

1984   Contributes interview chapter for *The Courage to Change*, a book on alcoholism by Dennis Wholey.

1986   Contributes sketch (co-written with Douglas Adams) to *The Utterly, Utterly Merry Comic Relief Christmas Book*.

1987   Guest appearances on "Still Crazy Like a Fox," CBS TV.

Hosts four episodes of "The Dangerous Film Club," TV series for Cinemax.

Writes (with D. Sherlock) and shoots pilot episode of "Jake's Journey" (sitcom) CBS TV, directed by Hal Ashby. CBS passes, but the Disney Channel picks up the option.

House is burgled. Among the items stolen are a computer with nearly completed manuscript of *A Liar's Autobiography, Part II* on it.

1988   Undertakes a lecture tour of U.S. college campuses.

June 11: Helps M.C. Artists Against Apartheid's "70th Birthday Tribute To Nelson Mandela" concert, Wembley Stadium, London.

November: A routine visit to the dentist turns tragic when a cancerous spot is discovered on his tonsils. Begins cancer treatment.

1989   Revives *Ditto* film project, rewriting script with David Sherlock.

Signs production deal with Ron Howard's Imagine Entertainment.

Records *A Liar's Autobiography* for Dove Audio (owned at that time by old friend Harry Nilsson).

Cancer treatment appears to be working, and Graham is released from hospital.

September: Reunites with the other Pythons for a cameo in "Parrot Sketch Not Included" (a.k.a. "20 Odd Years of Python"), a 20th anniversary salute to the team. There is talk of future Python activities, but this proves to be Graham's final public appearance.

October: Suffers a sudden relapse.

October 4: Dies of throat cancer in London, just one day shy of the team's 20th anniversary. Terry Jones calls it "The worst case of party-pooping I've ever seen."

Having been stuck by a needle and uttering an expletive, his last words (to the nurse) were: "Sorry about saying, 'Fuck'."